TALKS WITH AMERICAN STUDENTS

TALKS WITH
AMERICAN STUDENTS

J. KRISHNAMURTI

SHAMBHALA
BOSTON & SHAFTESBURY
1988

Shambhala Publications, Inc.

Horticultural Hall
300 Massachusetts Avenue
Boston, Massachusetts 02115

The Old School House
The Courtyard, Bell Street
Shaftesbury, Dorset SP7 8BP

10 9 8 7 6 5 4 3 2

Printed in the United States of America

Distributed in the United States by Random House
and in Canada by Random House of Canada Ltd.

Distributed in the United Kingdom by Element Books Ltd.

Library of Congress Cataloging-in-Publication Data
Krishnamurti, J. (Jiddu), 1895–1986.
    Talks with American students.
    Originally published: Talks with American students,
1968. Wassenaar, The Netherlands: Servire, 1970.
    Talks delivered in the United States and Puerto
Rico during 1968.
    1. Conduct of life. I. Title.
BJ1581.2.K759   1988   181'.4   88-15820
ISBN 0-87773-021-0 (pbk.)

CONTENTS

TALKS AT THE UNIVERSITY OF PUERTO RICO,
SAN JUAN

1

MOST OF US in this confused and brutal world try to carve
out a private life of our own, a life in which we can be happy
and peaceful and yet live with the things of this world. We
seem to think that the daily life we lead, the life of struggle,
conflict, pain and sorrow, is something separate from the
outer world of misery and confusion. We seem to think the
individual, the 'you', is different from the rest of the world
with all its atrocities, wars and riots, inequality and injustice
and that this is something entirely different from our particular individual life. When you look a little more closely, not
only at your own life but also at the world, you will see that
what you are — your daily life, what you think, what you
feel — *is* the external world, the world about you. You are
the world, you are the human being that has made this world
of utter disorder, the world that is crying helplessly in great
sorrow. It is you, the human being that has built this world.
So that world outside you is not different from the world in
which you live your private life.

This division between the individual and society does not
really exist at all. When one tries to carve out a life of one's
own, the individual is not different from the community in
which he lives. For the individual, the human being, has
constructed the community, society. I think we ought to be
very clear from the beginning that this division is artificial,
utterly unreal.

In bringing about a radical change in the human being,
in you, you are naturally bringing about a radical change in

the structure and the nature of society. I think it must be very clearly understood, that the human mind, with all its complexity, its intricate work, is part of this external world. The 'you' is the world and, in bringing about a fundamental revolution — neither Communist, nor socialist, but a totally different kind of revolution, within the very structure and nature of the psyche, of yourself — you will bring about a social revolution. It must begin, not outwardly but inwardly, because the outer is the result of our private, inner life.

When there is a radical revolution in the very nature of thought, feeling and action, then obviously there will be a change in the structure of society. This complete change in the structure of society must come about. Social morality is not moral. To be completely moral one must deny social morality. This means that the individual, the 'you' has to go into the whole structure of himself; he must understand himself, not according to any philosopher, nor priest, nor analyst, whoever he may be. He must understand himself as he is, not according to somebody else. When we understand ourselves, the authority of any specialist, psychosociological or any other, comes to an end. I feel this must be understood by each one of us before we go any further. Because most of us, unfortunately, are slaves to other people's ideas. Most of us are so easily persuaded, influenced by the specialist, by authority. Especially when we are going into this question of understanding ourselves, which is of primary importance, there is no authority whatsoever, because you have to understand yourself and not somebody else or what somebody else says about you. I think this is really a very important thing to grasp, because, as I said just now, we easily accept, we so easily obey, conform, and acquiesce in authority, whether it is the authority of the Church or of some spiritual leader or some analytical specialist. I think one has to discard all that, totally, because the authority that has been exercised and the obedience on the part of each one of us to a conceptual ideal, has brought about a great deal of misery in the world.

I do not know if you have observed how the world is divided into nationalities, religious groups, various categories of races, prejudices, with one religion against another, one God opposed to another God. You must have observed this. And yet having observed, knowing how this creates misery, conflict and division throughout the world, you go on adhering to your particular nationality, your particular religious concepts, your beliefs which all bring about division between man and man. Unfortunately, we accept the authority established by the tradition of society or the Church, the dictates of the authoritarian hierarchy of organised religion. But we do refuse to accept political tyranny. We do not accept that anybody should deny us the right to speak freely or to think what we wish to think. Unfortunately we do not exercise that same freedom with regard to spiritual matters. This has led throughout the world to untold misery and division among people.

If we would understand ourselves, which is absolutely essential — because without understanding ourselves we have no basis for thought or for clear perception — if we want to think rationally, sanely, we have to know ourselves, we have to search out the causes which make us think and do certain things, to find out why we are aggressive, brutal, acquisitive, dominating, possessive, as these characteristics are all causes of conflict between human beings. And when we wish to bring about a social change, which must take place, surely it must begin in the human mind, not in the outward structure of society. Once again, this must be clearly understood, that to bring about a radical change in the social structure — so that human beings can be free, so that there are no more wars, no more division of peoples into Christians, Hindus, Muslims and so on — there must be true self-understanding, through understanding ourselves, how we are made, both biologically and psychologically. Then in the very process of understanding ourselves we shall bring about a change which will be natural, not a bloody revolution. All political, religious and economic revolutions, have produced great misery and confusion in the world. You see what is going on in the Communist world, the repression, and the return to a bourgeois state.

Seeing all this, wars, tyranny, oppression, social injustice, starvation in the East, contrasted with extreme riches, seeing all this, not merely intellectually but actually, observing it in yourself, in your daily life, you must inevitably see that there must be a radical revolution in the very activity of your daily existence. And to bring about such a change there must be self-knowledge — knowing yourself as you are, the causes of your actions, why you are aggressive, brutal, envious, full of hate, which expresses itself in the outer world. I hope this is clear, not only logically, verbally, rationally, but also because you feel it. If you do not feel acutely, intensely, the actual state of the world, the actual state of your own life, then there is escape into ideologies and theories.

You know, ideologies have no meaning whatsoever, whether they are Communist, socialist, capitalist, or religious. Ideologies — conceptual thinking with its words — have separated man and man. You all have different ideologies, and do not see clearly for yourselves the idiocy of having ideologies. They prevent seeing what actually takes place, what actually is. Why should we have ideologies of any kind, knowing how they have divided man against man, whether of Christian, Hindu, Muslim or any other religion, each holding desperately to his belief? Why? We never question, we accept ideologies. If you question and probe deeply into this problem of ideologies you will see that they exist in order to escape from the actual.

Take for instance the whole question of violence, which

11

is spreading throughout the world at an astonishing speed. We are violent: human beings, right through the world are violent, aggressive, brutal. That is a fact, derived, inherited from the animal world. We are violent people. We do not deal with that violence, we do not find out why we are violent and go beyond it. But we have ideas about violence, ideologies about it. We say that we should be non-violent, we should be kind, we should be gentle, we should be tender and so on; this is merely conceptual thinking, which prevents us from coming into contact with ourselves when we are violent. That is fairly clear, isn't it?

We are asking why human beings indulge in ideals, and we think it is a most extraordinary thing if we do not have ideals. To live without a principle — please listen to this carefully — to live without principles, to live without beliefs, to live without ideals, you think is very worldly, that it is materialistic. On the contrary, those of you who have ideals, beliefs, principles, are the most materialistic people in the world, because you are not dealing with actuality, you are not dealing with violence, you are not dealing with facts as they are. I am sure many of you believe in God, although some of you may not. You may say you are an atheist, which is another form of belief. You never question why you believe in God; you accept Him because this is part of tradition, part of the authority of propaganda, you have this ideal and say, 'Your God and my God, your particular form of ritual and mine'. These beliefs and rituals have divided man. To find out reality, to find out if there is such a thing as God, to find out, to discover it, to experience it, to come upon that extraordinary state, one must completely set aside every form of belief. Otherwise one is not free to find out and it is only a mind that is free to enquire, to observe, that can come upon that reality which is not put together by the mind in fear.

Why does one have these many ideals and principles according to which one tries to live? In modern times people do not very much bother about principles and beliefs. In the modern world one is concerned with having a very good time, getting on, having success and so on. But when you go into the matter more deeply, you will see that fear is at the bottom of all this. It is fear that makes us aggressive. It is fear that demands that you have an escape through ideals. And it is fear that makes us hold on to our particular form of security in belief. If a man is not frightened, if a man lives completely, totally, without any contradiction within himself, observing the world with all its contradiction within himself, observing the world with all its brutality, and so going within himself and ridding himself of fear, then he can live without a single belief, a single conceptual thought. And I think that is the principle feature of our life: fear, not only fear of such things as losing a job but the fear of being psychologically, inwardly insecure.

I want now to say something which I consider important; it matters very much *how* you listen. Either you listen to words, intellectually, agreeing or disagreeing, or you listen with a mind that is interpretative, translating what you hear according to your own particular prejudices. You listen comparatively, that is you compare what you hear with what you already know. All listening of this kind obviously prevents you from listening. Doesn't it? If you say, 'Well! what you are talking about is nonsense', you are not listening. After all, you have come here and I have come here to talk things over together, to listen. And if you have your own particular prejudices, conclusions, definite opinions, which prevent you from listening to the speaker, then you will go away with a lot of words which have no meaning at all. Whereas, if you listen, without condemning or accepting, listen with a certain quality of attention, as you listen to the wind among the trees, if you listen with your whole being, with your heart and with your mind, then perhaps we shall establish communication between ourselves. Then we shall understand each other very simply and very directly, although we are dealing with a very complex human problem. We are concerned with the whole structure of our daily life, we are involved with our sorrow, with our misery, with struggle and pain. And if we know how to listen, not only to the speaker now, but also when we go home, then we shall be actually listening to wife, husband, children, or anyone else, then we shall begin to discover for ourselves the truth of the matter. The mind then becomes very simple and clear; it becomes a very clear mind, which can observe, and learn, is not confused or frightened. And we have very complex problems. Our life is very complex and to understand this very complex structure of ourselves we need to observe ourselves very closely, to see why we believe, why we hate, why we are aggressive, why we separate ourselves into nationalities.

So as I said, if you would listen with care, with that quality of affection which is attention, then you will see that what the speaker is speaking about *is* the discovery of yourself. The speaker is merely painting a picture of yourself. To observe that picture you have to give attention, care, neither condemning, nor justifying, nor being ashamed of what you see. It is only by seeing what is actually taking place in your life and observing it very closely, without any condemnation, or evaluation, that you will see it as it is. To see is the greatest miracle. Please see that. We do not see because we look at ourselves with eyes that are always condemning, comparing, evaluating, and therefore we never see ourselves as we are. And to see ourselves as we are is to bring about a radical change in ourselves, and therefore in the social order and structure.

In ourselves we are very confused and disorderly. There is no order within us. I do not mean the seeming order obtained by imitating and conforming; this is disorder, and you can see for yourselves that life is fragmentary, broken up.

You are a businessman, you are a husband, you are a wife, you are this and that, your life is broken up in fragments. Each fragment has its own desire, its own purpose, motive, one in opposition to the other, and so there is contradiction. Our life is a contradiction, one desire in opposition to the other desire, one pleasure pulling us in one direction and another pleasure pulling us in another, making our life contradictory, confused and disorderly. That is an obvious fact, and we have to bring about order, not according to some blueprint, or according to some theory, but according to that order which comes into being when we observe the causes of disorder in ourselves. I hope I am making this clear. This is not a question of rhetoric or theories, we are concerned with what is actually taking place in ourselves. Because in ourselves is the world. We cannot separate ourselves from the world. We are the world. And to change the world — and there must be change — one must change oneself. To bring about an orderly change we must understand the causes of the disorder that exists in us; and that is all. We have nothing more to do than to observe the causes of disorder in ourselves.

To observe there must be freedom. You know, most of us are very heavily conditioned by the society in which we live, by the culture in which we have grown up. The society in which we live is the product of our life, of our way of thinking. Culture is what we have made. Society has conditioned us, has told us what to think and how to think, what our beliefs must be and how we must behave. We are heavily conditioned and therefore we are not free. This is an actual, obvious fact. With a conditioned mind we are obviously not free to observe. And, being conditioned, when we observe the actual state we are in we are frightened. We do not know what to do. The question then is whether it is at all possible for the human mind to uncondition itself — please listen to this — for the human mind to uncondition itself so that it can

15

be free. If you say it is not possible, that no human mind can ever be free of its conditioning, then you have blocked yourself, you have prevented further investigation into the problem. And if you say it is possible, that again blocks you, prevents you from examining the question.

So, to understand this conditioning — it is clear what we mean by that word 'conditioning' — you are conditioned as a Christian, you have been brought up in a particular culture, a culture that accepts war, that pursues a particular pattern of existence and so on. That is your conditioning in the same way as people in India are conditioned by their culture, their religion and superstition, their way of life. And that word 'conditioning' is a very clear, simple word with a great depth of meaning.

Now, is it possible to uncondition the mind, uncondition your mind so that it is free? You know, freedom is one of the most dangerous things, because freedom implies for most people that they can do what they want to do. Freedom for most people is an ideal, it is something far away, it cannot be had. And there are those who say, to be free you must be greatly disciplined. But freedom is not at the end; freedom is at the very first step. If you are not free you cannot observe the tree, the clouds, the flashing waters, you cannot observe your relationship with your wife, your husband, or your neighbour. Most of us do not want to observe, because we are frightened of what will happen if we observe very closely.

I do not know if you have ever observed your relationships, for instance your relationship with your wife or your husband. This is a very dangerous subject. Because if we observe very closely we see that there must be a different kind of life that we never observe. What we observe is the image that we have built about each other and that image establishes a certain relationship between man and woman. That relationship between the images is what we regard as being in contact, being in relation with another. So when we are enquiring into this question of unconditioning, freeing the mind from its own conditioning, first of all, we want to know if this is possible. If it is not possible then we are forever slaves. If it is not possible then we invent a heaven, a God. In heaven alone we can be free, but not here. And to free the mind from its conditioning — and I say this is possible, it can be done — we must become aware, aware of how we think, and why we think, and what our thoughts are. To be aware — not to condemn, not to judge but just to observe, as one observes a flower. It is there in front of you — it is no good your condemning it, it is no use your saying 'I like it' or 'I dislike it' — it is there, for you to look at. And if you have the eyes to see you will see the beauty of that flower. In the same way, if you are aware of yourself, without condemning, without judging, then you will see the whole structure and the cause of your conditioning; if you pursue it deeply, then you will discover for yourself that the mind can be free.

This brings to view another problem: we are used to thinking in terms of time, that is, we are used to the gradual process of change, the gradual process of achievement, the time involved in changing from this to that. That is time. There is time not only by the watch, chronologically, but there is also psychological time, the inward time, which says, 'I am angry, jealous, and I will gradually get over this'. That constitutes gradation, the slow process of change, but there is no such thing psychologically, inwardly, as gradualness. Either you change immediately or you do not change at all. To change gradually from violence to non-violence implies that you are sowing the seed of violence all the time, doesn't it? If I say to myself that being violent I will gradually, some day, become non-violent, time is involved. In that interval of time I am continually sowing the seeds of violence; this is very obvious.

So, the question is, speaking very seriously in a world that is disrupted, is shattering itself, and is distracted by amusement, this question is one not only of time but of the whole conflict of effort. I hope this is not becoming too difficult? Perhaps it is, if we are not used to this kind of intensive thinking and feeling. But there it is, and it's up to you. You see, when a house is burning, as our house — our world — is burning, you do not discuss about theories, nor ask who set it on fire, (Communist, capitalist, socialist or the Catholics or the Protestants or anything). You are concerned with putting out the fire and seeing to it that you build a house that can never be set on fire again. And that demands great seriousness and intensity, not merely engaging in action for action's sake or doing some good or making some change from one religion or one concept to another.

So, one has to be serious and this means being free to observe life, to observe the way of your life, to observe your relationship with others, and to see very clearly what is happening. You know, you cannot observe if there is space between you and the thing observed. Does that make any sense to you? I will show you what I mean. To observe, to see very clearly, you must be very closely in contact with the thing you observe. You must be able to touch it, you must be able to feel it, you must be able to be completely in contact with it. And if there is a space between you, the observer, and the thing observed, then you are not in contact. So, to observe yourself as you are — please listen to this, just listen — to observe yourself there must be no division between the observer and the thing observed. Does this make sense? You will see it. If I look at myself and there is a separation between myself and the thing observed, and I see that I am jealous, angry, violent, the observer and the thing observed are two different things, aren't they? There is violence and the observer who says 'I am violent'. They are two different things. This separation between the observer and the thing observed causes conflict. Do watch it in yourself and you

18

will understand it very simply. If you separate yourself from fear then you must overcome it, you must fight it, you must struggle against it, you must escape from it. But when you see that you *are* the fear, that the observer is the observed, then the conflict between the two comes to an end. And when the observer is the observed then time comes to an end.

What we are saying is, man has travelled for so long, his life is a battlefield, not only within himself but outwardly, all his relationships are in conflict, in the factory, in the office, at home, it is a constant struggle and battle. And we are saying that such a life is no life at all. You may have your gods, you may have your riches, you may have an extraordinary capacity, but you are not living, you are not happy people. There is no happiness, no bliss in life. And to come upon this happiness, this bliss, one must understand oneself, and to understand oneself there must be freedom to look. To look properly there must be no division between the observer and the observed. And when this takes place, this whole sense of struggle to become something, to be something, disappears. You are what you are. In observing this, there comes an immediate, radical change. That puts an end to the idea of time and gradualness.

10th September 1968

2

WE WERE SAYING the other day that our whole relationship with other human beings must undergo a radical change. All over the world, frightening violence is spreading. Wars, racial riots and conflict exist outside of our skin and inside it. Our life is a battlefield, a constant struggle, from the moment we are born till we die, and we hope somewhere in this battlefield to find some kind of peace, some place where we can take refuge. That is more or less what man is seeking all the time, a certain refuge outwardly, in society, and some security inwardly. This is one of the major causes of conflict, this demand on the part of every human being right throughout the world to find some kind of resting-place, some kind of relationship in which there is no longer any conflict, some kind of ideology that would be assuring and lasting. So man begins to invent an ideology of religion, of organized belief, of dogma, which will give him deep, satisfying hope. But as one can see throughout the world, organized religion, like nationality, divides people. There have been untold wars in the name of God, in the name of religion, in the name of peace, in the name of freedom. And I think one must realise that every form of relationship must inevitably lead to chaos and conflict, if it is based on conceptual thinking. We went into that the last time that we met here. Man has tried to find some kind of reality that will be completely true — not be an invention of the mind — something that will give significance to life, a meaning to the drab existence of every-day life. I think that is what most people, both intellectual and so-called religious people are always trying to find — a meaning to life. Because our life as it is now is pretty drab and meaningless, with little pleasures, little satisfactions, sexual and otherwise. But man demands much more, something truer, deeper, with more meaning.

So he begins to invent or give a significance to life, intellectually or conceptually; this again fails, as it is merely an invention, a theory, a possibility. It is no good trying to find something that is really true, not an invention, nor a concept but an actuality, a reality that can never be destroyed by thought. To come upon that one must establish right relationship in this world, right human relationship, a right society, a structure of society, culture, that gives man opportunity to live here fully, that will make life agreeable, happy, a life in which there is no conflict, a life that is truly moral. And it is only then when the foundation is laid rightly, that there is a possibility of finding out for oneself what is truth.

Our concern must be to live completely and totally in this world, to live so that our relationship with our neighbours — whether a thousand miles away or next door — does not breed conflict. There will have to be a society which is not competitive, brutal, aggressive, destructive, a society which does not breed wars. Society is the outcome of our daily life — whatever we are in our daily life, the way we act, the things to which we give value, how we behave, our daily conduct — all this breeds a society in which there must be war, hate, antagonism. So we have to find out for ourselves (not according to any moralist) how to live so completely, totally, and at the same time morally, to live so freely as human beings, completely at peace within ourselves, that a society comes about in which all the clashes of racial and economic differences disappear and there can be equal opportunity for every human being. That will only be possible if each one of us human beings feels the complete necessity of living so that his life is an expression of peace and freedom. That is the real question, whether we can, living in this society, change it — not through violent means, because that has never produced a society based on freedom and peace — make it into a society which gives man freedom, so that he is a light to himself.

So our question is, society as it exists must be changed. That is obvious. The Communists have not been able to do it, though they have murdered thousands, millions of people. The capitalists also have not been able to do it. So one must find a different way of living — not a system, socialistic or any other kind of system — but a different way of living. And that can come about only as we said the other day, when we understand ourselves, not merely as individuals but in relationship with society. Because we are society, we are the world, it is not something different from us. The culture which conditions you, the society which binds you, shapes you, is your struggle, your way of life. So our question is whether it is possible to change our everyday life so radically, so fundamentally that our whole thinking process is different? We are by nature, through inheritance, instinct, violent people. We are very self-centred — me first and everything else second — my security, my position, my prestige is much more important than anybody else's, and this breeds the competitive spirit, which has produced society, with all its racial and economic divisions. So unless there is a deep change in the psyche itself, mere outward reformation through bloodshed and legislation, will not bring about ultimately a way of life in which man is at peace within himself, in which he can live virtuously, a life in which he can seek and find reality.

After all, we are all seeking happiness. But happiness is a by-product, is a result, not an end in itself. Our problem is, how is it possible to change man? Is it through an analytical process, going into the question of the cause of his behaviour, of his violence, of his aggression, analysing it very, very carefully to find out the causes, and then through gradual time, through gradual process, during many years, to bring about a change? Is that the way? Do you understand the question? That is, will each one of us as human beings change totally our ways of life through the understanding of the causes of our behaviour, both publicly and privately, secretly and openly, to find out the causes of why we are aggressive, why we are competitive, why we are violent? If we analyse very carefully, step by step, so that no mistakes are made, will that bring about a change? That analytical process implies time, doesn't it? It will take many days, perhaps many years to analyse very, very carefully. And perhaps through willing it, then we might change. But I doubt it. Man has never changed, though he knows the cause of violence, though he has experienced thousands of wars, he has not stopped killing. He kills animals for his food and he kills people for ideologies.

If we take time it will take many years to change — please go into this with me, do not merely listen to what I say as to a series of ideas — we are not concerned with ideas, we are concerned with daily living and bringing about a radical change in that living. And so, do not please merely agree or disagree, refuting or accepting. As we said the other day, one has to listen very attentively, not to the speaker but using the speaker as a mirror in which one sees oneself, so that one becomes aware of oneself. So our question is, will the analytical process free the mind? This implies time; chronologically it may take many days, many years. It will do so if you go into it analytically. And, as it takes many years you will be helping to bring about chaos in the world, more wars, more aggression. So, that is not the way. The analytical process, based on the discovery of the causes of human behaviour implies time and we have no time, when the house is burning, when there is such brutal existence, when there is so much hate; when the house is on fire, you have no time, you have to change immediately; that is the real question. The intellectual process, which is the analytical process, is not the way. And the religious people say, right throughout the world in their own phraseology, you must wait for the grace of God, which again is absurd. Then there must be a totally different way, for man, realizing the condition of the world, observing what is actually going on, not theoretically nor intellectually, but seeing the violence, the brutality, the hatred, the wars, the killing, for which he is responsible. Look at the war that is going on in Vietnam; each one of us is responsible for it. Each one of us is also responsible for the riots and the racial prejudices. You live in this happy island with the lovely green hills and the blue sea, seemingly isolated, but you are not so, you are part of the world, part of this terrible misery that is going on. And when you see that, you also see that to go into the analytical process using the intellectual way of examining, does not answer the problem at all. Neither the religious outlook, nor the bloody revolution, bringing about anarchy in the world, solves this question.

So, there must be a different way of bringing about an immediate change in the mind. Perhaps you will say that it is not possible. You will say, 'I, who am so conditioned by society, conditioned by the culture in which I live, am so heavily bound that it is not possible for me to change instantly'. To give up smoking, for example, is something you find very difficult. And to give up, to put aside complex ideological conditioning is immensely more difficult. So you say it is not possible to free the mind instantly and be free of every kind of antagonism, brutality, violence. I think it is possible, not as an idea, not as an Utopian theory, but actually. Is it possible for the human mind, conditioned for millions of years, to change, radically, instantly? Now I will show what I mean. We will discuss it. First of all, all thought, all thinking, is the result of the past, as all knowledge is of the past. All thinking is the response of memory and memory always belongs to yesterday. You can observe this for your-selves, it is not some mystical nonsense, it is a scientific fact which you can observe for yourself when you ask a question. Your mind looks into what you already know, into the memory, and then according to that memory it responds. I am putting it very quickly and briefly, because it is a very complex problem. Thought is always conditioned, and thought is always old. And here is a new problem, totally new, a new challenge which says, you must change immedi-ately, otherwise you are going to destroy yourself. And to that challenge, naturally, the reaction is that of the old. If you respond to it according to the old systems of thought, then you are not acting adequately to that challenge. I hope this is clear.

And so, to this new challenge which demands that you change instantly — because the alternative is that you are going to destroy yourself, because you know that there are more wars coming, more brutality, more suppressions, that the extreme Left is becoming rampant and the extreme Right is getting stronger, and that this will lead to more bloodshed, more wars, more hatred — seeing all that objectively you come to the inevitable conclusion that the human mind must change integrally, totally, immediately. And thought cannot do this because thought is the response of the past. And when you respond to something new according to the old, there is no communication between the new challenge and yourself. I do not know if this is clear.

The new challenge to human beings who have lived for so long in such misery which is now increased by dreadful destructive instruments, the challenge is that you must change instantly. And if your response is not new, you will be in greater conflict, you will be contributing to greater sorrows for men. So you must respond to the new challenge in a new way. And that is only possible when you understand the whole structure and nature of thought. If you respond intellectually, verbally, conceptually, then it is the operation and the approach of the old. So, is it possible — please listen to this, however absurd it may sound, please listen to it first — is it possible to respond without thought, respond with your whole being and not part of your being? Thought or the intellect is a fragment of your whole being, obviously, and when a partial, a fragmentary part answers to an immense challenge, it creates more conflict. So thought, the intellect, as it is a fragment of the total human being will not produce a radical change, it is not the means of approaching this challenge. It is only when the totality of the human mind — mind being the nervous responses, the emotions, the everything that is you — completely responds, without any fragmentation in that response, that there is a new action taking place. If I respond to this challenge intellectually, verbally, it will only be a fragmentary response, it will not be a total, human response. And the total human response is only possible when I give my mind and heart to it completely. That is, the response to the new challenge to be adequate, to be complete, is one unique response, which is not intellectual, nor verbal, nor theoretical; and that response is (if I may use that word which has been so spoilt) love.

You know, that word has been so spoilt by us, spoilt by the priests, by the politicians, by the husband and the wife, spoilt in such a way that when we say that we love God — we do not. We speak of love of country, love of the ideal, and that word has become ugly. If we can strip that word of all the ugliness, then we can see what that word means. Because when you love you love totally, completely with all your being. And love is not pleasure. For most of us, for most human beings, love implies pleasure, sexual or otherwise. And we have spoilt that word by characterising it as divine and not divine. But love is something that must be grasped, understood, lived and felt, with no fragmentation into intellect, emotion, physical love and so on. It is a total

26

response. And it is only that response that brings about a radical revolution in the mind. I think for the time being that is enough from me, so will you ask questions? Shall we talk about it?

But, before you ask questions, may I ask you to make them brief, and to the point, because I have to repeat your questions. And if I repeat your question wrongly, please tell me. If you speak Italian, French, Spanish or English of course, I may be able to understand. So please make it brief and to the point and referring to what we are talking about, not some theoretical question, but how to bring about a fundamental change in man. Sir?

Questioner: How can you communicate this feeling or this word love, this meaning behind the word love to others?

KRISHNAMURTI: How can you communicate with the world, with the rest of the group? Is that the question, Sir? Do not bother to communicate with others. Have this thing. You know, we are so eager to communicate our findings to others, we want to convince others, we want to tell them; this is not a question of propaganda, this is not a thing that you can just propagate by word, you can only tell it to others by your life, the way you live every day. If a hundred people in this room really understood it, lived it — good God! Sir, a flower which is full of nectar, full of beauty and colour is not bothered about propagating itself, isn't concerned with anything — it is what it is. And if you are sensitive and alive and capable of looking at that flower, that is enough. So what matters is not the other, the person that is not here, what matters is the person that is here.

Questioner: What makes love true for human beings?

KRISHNAMURTI: It is fairly simple, isn't it? If you are jealous, this is obviously not love. If there is fear there is obviously

27

no love. If you are dominating somebody else, it is not love. If you talk about love and go to the office and cause harm to others, it is not love. So when you know what is not love and put it aside, not theoretically but actually in your life, and when there is neither hate nor fear, then the other is.

Questioner: Should we not love ourselves first?

KRISHNAMURTI: I am afraid we do. *(laughter)* And that is the bane of it. Our love for ourselves is so great, we are so self-centred, we love our country, our God, our beliefs, our dogmas, our possessions, and these are ourselves. Look at the mess this has brought about in the world. I do not think we see the gravity or the seriousness of what is going on in the world and we do not seem to be aware of our own lives. We live them in a routine way, in boredom and the fear of loneliness and of not being loved. And so our actions produce hatred and antagonism. We are not aware of all this. And religions with their organized beliefs have merely helped us to escape from our daily life, preventing us from looking. Love is something that you cannot talk about. You know what it is not. And when you go into it and put aside in yourself what it is not, then it is.

Questioner: There is fear of slander ... the Zen Buddhists say that you must die every day and that then perhaps you may find reality.

KRISHNAMURTI: I wonder why you bother to repeat what other people say. What Zen Buddhists say or what the Hindus say or what the Christian Bible says or what the specialists say; must you have this authority? Do think about it, please. We are second-hand people, we repeat what others say, what Zen, what the Vedanta, what Yoga teaches and so on. We are never a light to ourselves. We are such mediocre people. So, the questioner says, by dying each day one comes upon reality. Do you know what that means? Do you know what it means to die to anything, to die to some pleasure that you cherish? Have you ever tried? You know, one has to go very deeply into this question and it is quite complex. A mind that is continuous, that repeats, that is caught in habits, that functions as a conditioned mind, anything that has continuity, cannot see anything new. It is only when there is an ending, a total ending that something new can be perceived. And to die to our pleasure, to a particular form of memory, is almost impossible for most human beings.

You know, this question brings in a much larger one which is the question of death. I do not know if this is the time or this is the occasion to talk about it. Because we have very few minutes left. But perhaps when we meet here again we might go into it. And to understand what death is one must understand what living is. We don't understand what living is; for us living is a battlefield, conflict, brutality, sometimes at rare intervals a flash of joy and happiness. That is what we call living. If we do not understand what living is how can we understand what dying is. We are frightened of living and we are frightened of dying. And Zen, that is, a certain form of meditation says that you must die every day. Of course one must die every day and there is beauty in that, because everything then is new. That means dying to all experience. Again we have not time to go into that now and I hope you will not mind this. Perhaps next time we meet we shall go into it.

Questioner: Is God participating in our lives and if that isn't so what can we do about it?

KRISHNAMURTI: Now this is again one of the most complex questions. Like every human question it is very complex. You know, you do believe in God. Somebody says, 'I am God'. There are two things here aren't there; why do you believe in God and if you say, 'I am God', do you mean it, or, is it just an idea? Just look at it. Find out

29

what the truth of it is, not what you believe and what I believe. Belief has no reality in the face of what is true. To find out what God (or whatever is there) truly is, there must be no fear, there must be no sense of possession, acquisitiveness, envy — do you follow? — there must be complete virtue. A flowering of goodness, that is the foundation, not what you believe or what your religion is, what your conditioning or what propaganda tells you that there is or there is not. If you intend to say, 'I am God', don't say it, because you do not know what you are saying. That is one of the sayings of the Hindus in India, that they are God, only covered up by matter, by manifestation of this world and this is too complex. To find out if there is reality, don't assert anything, don't assert anything, don't belong to any group, to any belief. One must be free to find out, like a scientist is, a really good scientist, not one who is merely using his capacity to further mischief, but the true scientist. The true scientist is free to examine, without any bias, without any conditioning, to look. If we approach things in this way and, if we are lucky, we may find out what reality is. No conceptual assertion that there is or that there is not comes into it. That requires great love and beauty; it demands humility. And when we say that there is God, or that there is no God, this is utter lack of humility.

Questioner: Are fear and evasion the same thing?

KRISHNAMURTI: He is saying, 'You have an image of fear and an image of the psyche, of the 'me'; there is the image of myself and the image I have about fear'. Now, are the two things different? You understand the question? There is the image of myself — 'I must be good, or I am not good, I am ashamed, I am frightened' and all that, and I create another image in which there are the various attributes of myself. Look, let us put it very simply. You have an image about your wife or your husband, don't you? You must, obviously.

Is the image that you have about your wife, or your wife about her husband, different from yourself? Please follow this. The image you have about yourself has been put together through experience and the image you have about your wife or your husband has been put together in the same way. So experience is the imagemaker. Are you following? Am I making myself fairly clear? Now, experience is the factor that makes my images about myself and about my wife, and my wife does the same about me. This image-making is brought about through experience. But to be related to a human being implies being in relationship with another human being without an image, and the absence of image means the absence of experience. Experience has built, put together the image about myself and experience has put together the image about my wife and hers about me. To be actually in relationship with human beings is to have no image. This is not a theory — see it as you see this microphone, objectively, factually. This means that whatever my wife says to me in anger or in pleasure or in affection, must leave no residue, it must leave no mark, otherwise it becomes an experience. I wonder if you are catching this. If she says to me something pleasant, I like it. That is an experience which I cherish, and I hold on to it. And that creates an image about my wife. And that creates also an image of my own delight.

Now, if my wife tells me something ugly, that also creates an image. The question then is: is it possible, when she tells me something pleasant, to look at it so completely, so fully that it leaves no experience at all? Are you following all this? To live that way demands great attention, and awareness, whether she insults or flatters, nags or dominates me, or whether I dominate her. In this way my relationship is always fresh, is always new; otherwise it is not real relationship, it is only a relationship between two images, and this has no validity at all. The images in that case are symbols and having

31

a relationship between two symbols is meaningless. But that is how we live, in a meaningless relationship — I am sorry to expose it so brutally — in which there is no love. Love is something always fresh, new, young, innocent.

Questioner: When a person establishes a goal for himself and pursues that, how can he not be conditioned?

KRISHNAMURTI: I do not know why you want goals. A goal implies distance, something in the future. You have established that goal as a purpose and you are conforming all your life, battling with yourself to conform to that pattern. That is what you mean by a goal, don't you? An end, a purpose, a goal is something in the distance which you have established for yourself; it may be an image, it may be an idea, it may be an ideology, a noble one at that. But, first of all, why do you want goals at all? You see, you can't answer that. Wait, I must finish this question, Sir.

Questioner: Do we need goals?

KRISHNAMURTI: Yes, Sir, that's right. We need goals because we are conditioned, we have to aim at something. Why do you do that? I know we are conditioned, but why? Can't you go into it a little bit more deeply?

Questioner: Because we are not perfect we make perfection the goal.

KRISHNAMURTI: Look at it, please do look at it! You have the image of perfection which means that you are imperfect, now why do you want an image at all? You are imperfect aren't you and you want to change this. Why do you want a goal? 'I am imperfect'. What does that mean? I am angry, I am brutal, I am envious, I am frightened. Why do I want a goal, a goal, a perfection? Here is a fact. I am frightened; why can't I save myself from fear? But we want an ideal. Perfection is merely an escape from the imperfect. The

32

imperfect is also an image, as is the perfection. You don't see all this. So to live implies to live with 'what is' and bring about a radical change in what is. And that is not possible if you have a principle, a goal, an image of perfection. That is romanticism, that is not spiritual at all. What is spiritual is to see the fact as it is and change it. If I am violent I become aware of it, know the nature of it, the structure of it, the 'why'. And the very seeing of it, instantly is the ending of it.

Questioner: Could change be a goal in itself?

KRISHNAMURTI: No, Sir, look — when you have a toothache you want to end it, don't you? You don't have the idea or the image of perfect health, of having no pain at all; you have pain. That is the major factor, not the goal.

12th September 1968

3

ONE OF OUR great difficulties is that we never ask fundamental questions. And if we do ask them, we look to somebody else to answer them. We never find out for ourselves
the complete understanding of any problem. But perhaps this
evening we may have time to take three of four fundamental
problems, and see if we can answer them for ourselves,
neither depending on the speaker nor on anyone else. Most
of us accept authority too easily as we think that is the
easiest way. But, if one has observed, authority in these
matters invariably brings about a great deal of confusion and
contradiction. So there is no authority to tell us what to do
or how to think about fundamental questions. We are apt to
slur them over or pass them by, not being very deeply concerned by them. I will try to expose the fundamental questions and go into them. It is your responsibility to work as
hard as the speaker, to go into these questions intimately, for
yourself, and not to accept the authority of the speaker at a
single moment of time.

I think there are three fundamental problems, which if
we could answer or explore them in our own lives, by this
very exploration the confusions and sorrows of the world
might perhaps be answered. Then these questions may cease
to have the enormous importance that one now gives to them.
These fundamental questions are, what is living, what is
death, and what is life? We shall have to go into these questions very deeply and answer them for ourselves, because
they are a great challenge and we cannot possibly escape from
them. One has to answer them very seriously. And in ex-

ploring these issues, there must be first a quality of freedom to explore, to investigate, otherwise no one can possibly see or discover where the truth lies. One cannot have theories or ideologies. To find out the truth about these matters there must be freedom to look, to observe and to investigate. Otherwise we merely tread the path of tradition, authority and obedience, which has not in any way solved the problems of our life.

So, what is living? What does it mean to live? To find out what it means we must examine what living actually is. If we say that living should be this or that, then that is merely a supposition, a theory. Whereas, if we could look at what our life really is, the daily life that we live, year in and year out, if we could see it as it actually is, then we could deal with it, come to grips with it. But if we say it 'should be that', or think according to certain conditions, principles or ideologies, then we shall be wasting our time. Whereas if we could look at our life as it is, not as we would like it to be, then perhaps our life, as it is could be fundamentally altered. When we observe what it is, we can see that we are pursuing pleasure. To us, pleasure is one of the most important things, almost an essential thing. And pleasure is what most of us are seeking. Our values, morals, ethics, inward laws, are based on this pleasure principle. And when there is pleasure, and when we are seeking that as the highest form of existence, then there will be not only fear but also sorrow. Our whole life is concentrated in the pursuit of pleasure (as it is now) and we are not condemning this, we are merely looking at it, observing it, exploring why man everlastingly seeks pleasure.

What is pleasure? This must be answered by each one of us, and we must also find out why we seek pleasure, not saying that we should not seek it or that it must be suppressed. Why is it that most of us seek pleasure? And what is pleasure? Why should we seek or not seek pleasure? So there

35

are three questions in that. Our values are based on pleasure. And why is it that pleasure has become such an urgent, all-demanding pursuit. What is pleasure? (There is physical pleasure, having good health, sexual pleasure, pleasure of achievement, of success or of being somebody famous. Please do observe yourself, not merely listen to the speaker. Watch how your own mind invariably turns to pleasure). We have accepted pleasure as part of our life. Why is it that pleasure has become such an extraordinarily important thing? You know, life is a series of experiences. All the time we are having experiences, and we avoid any experience that gives us pain, or we resist it. And any experience that gives us pleasure we pursue, doggedly, earnestly. What is pleasure? How does it come about? You see a sunset, and when you see it, it gives you great delight. You experience it and that experience leaves a memory. That experience has been of great delight and pleasure, to look at that marvellous sunset, over the hills, with the clouds lighted up. That experience leaves a memory of pleasure and tomorrow you will want that pleasure repeated, it is not only a case of looking at the sunset but also of the pleasure that you have had through sex; all this you want to repeat. This repetition takes place, as you can observe, when thought thinks about it. You have seen that sunset and there is pleasure in it; thought thinks about it and gives it vitality, continuity. The same with sex, the same with other forms of physical and psychological pleasure. Thought thinks or creates the image of that pleasure and keeps on thinking about it. And thought also, as we observe, breeds fear. I am afraid of what is going to happen tomorrow. I am afraid of the things I did some years ago being discovered, thinking about what might happen in the future and what has happened in the past — which I do not like, of which I am ashamed — and this breeds fear.

So thought creates, gives continuity to pleasure as well as continuity to fear. That is obvious. So, thought breeds sorrow, invites sorrow and thought also searches out pleasure. So our life — which we live every day, apart from theories, apart from what we should do, apart from the religions we belong to, apart from ideologies — our life is a constant struggle between these two things, pleasure and fear. And our life, as we observe it, is full of sorrow, not only caused physically by pain, but also brought about psychologically, inwardly. So, our life, as it is, is the battle between pleasure, fear and sorrow. Our life is a conflict, a struggle, psychologically, inwardly, which is expressed outwardly as society. Our life, actually 'as it is' is constant contradiction, pain and sorrow, with occasional flashes of joy.

And one asks oneself — and I hope you ask yourself this too — whether such a life can end, with its hate, jealousy, envy, ambition, greed, whether it can be transformed into a different kind of life, of a different dimension. Can one die to all the past? For if you observe, pleasure is in the past or in the future. The actual moment of pleasure is translated in terms of the past or of tomorrow. I don't know if you ever observed this. And one asks oneself seriously whether it is possible to live a life in which there is no conflict at all, no conflict between pleasure and fear. Not that there is not pleasure when you see something beautiful — a sunset, a cloud, a lovely face, a tree in the moonlight — there is great delight in seeing such things, such experiences cannot be denied. But thought comes in and says: what a lovely thing that was, I must have it again. And so thought thinks about it, as it does with regard to pain and sorrow.

So the question is, whether thought, which gives continuity to pain and to pleasure, can stop giving sustenance to the past and the future as pleasure, pain, or fear. Am I making myself clear?

We were asking what the function of thought is. Thought has a reality, thought must function. In the whole of the technological field, in all inventions thought is extraordinarily important. The more one thinks clearly, logically, sanely, without any prejudice or sentimentality, thought has such extraordinary importance that without it one could not go to one's home; you could not go to your office; all the scientific, accumulated knowledge would come to an end, if we did not exercise thought. But has thought any other existence? You are following my question? I know I must think, to tell you something, to learn a new language, I must think, accumulate words, grammar and so on in order to use thought as a medium of expression. Thought is necessary. But psychologically, inwardly, has thought any place at all? Please, this is a very serious question. Why should thought interfere or give continuity to an experience that has given delight? You saw that sunset yersterday, a marvellous thing with extraordinary colours, vitality, beauty. You saw it, and that is the end of it. But why should thought come in and think about it and turn it into a pleasure which you want to be repeated tomorrow? When you look at it you want this thing and then you are not actually looking at the sunset. What you are looking at is the memory of the sunset which you enjoyed yesterday. It is exactly the same with sex, it is exactly the same with every form of pleasure.

And has thought, which breeds fear and sorrow and pleasure, any place psychologically, inwardly? Thought must exist, for our lives to function. But inwardly, psychologically as thought breeds pain, sorrow and this constant drive for pleasure — bringing its own frustrations, disappointments, anger, jealousy and envy — thought has no place at all in that dimension, at that level. If one could actually do this: only exercise thought when it is absolutely necessary, and the rest of the time, observe, look. So that thought which is always old, which now prevents the actual experience of looking, could drop away and it would be possible to live totally in that moment, which is always the 'now'.

The next issue we are going to talk over together is 'what

is death'? Why is the mind so afraid of dying. We are all going to die. Science may invent some medicine or other medical practice to give man a longer time to live in his wretched misery. But there is always death to follow. Nowadays nobody talks about it because they are too frightened. And we want to find out the truth of death, actually, to find out why thought has created this image of fear. You see there is our life, our life which is so ugly, messy, contradictory with its wars, destruction and hate. And if you have a talent, a skill of some kind which gives you great pleasure, in that there is also great pain. That is our life, and we are tuned to it. And thought says to itself: 'I do not know what death is. I will put it as far away from me as possible'. Being frightened of the unknown, it invents a great many theories. The whole Asiatic world believes in reincarnation, that is, being reborn, with all the complex theories involved in this. And the Christian world also has its own means of escape from the actual fact of death. The fear of it is created by thought, because thought says: 'I know only the past, the known, the everyday life, the memories, the remembrance of things, of pleasure and pain. I only know the past, the old. I do not know what is going to happen, tomorrow or in thirty years time. So I keep the idea of death as far away as possible.' And therefore thought is fragmented.

So is it possible to find out psychologically what it means to die. The physical organism, by constant usage, strain and so on will inevitably deteriorate, through disease, accident or old age. How strange it is, that we are so frightened of old age. That is what we are, aren't we? And as we grow old, how ugly we become, how we cover ourselves with jewels, with fanciful hair-dos and pretend that we are young again. There is great sadness in all this, because it means that we have never lived, we do not even know what living is, and we are therefore frightened of old age. So, is it possible, psychologically, to die to every thing we know? And that

39

is what is going to happen when we die. We are going to leave our family, our experiences, our ambitions, our achievements. God knows what else. We cannot argue with death, ask him to postpone the inevitable hour. We can escape by thinking about it and say, 'I will live hereafter or I will be resurrected or I will be this or that'. Those are just theories, fanciful, psychological concepts, without any reality.

But is it possible to die to every thing psychologically known? Have you ever tried it, to die to a pleasure, to die to a particular experience that you hold very dear, to drop it, easily, happily, without struggle. This would be a morbid, masochistic state, unless accomplished without effort. But, if you do not do this, you do not know what living is. Look at the terrible mess that we have made of life; the fragmentation, the ugliness, the brutality of it all. But if we could die, inwardly, to all attachments of family, position, achievement, then we should be free from the known which is always the past, projecting itself as the future, but still remaining the past. If we can die to the known then perhaps we shall know what it means to live. Living then becomes quite a different thing; it is then possible to create quite a different kind of society, different from this murderous society, full of injustice, wars and immorality. Because when you die to the known, then perhaps you will know what love is. Love is not the thing that we have now — jealous, envious, suspicious, intriguing, anxious and pleasure seeking. When there is real love, pleasure is quite a different thing. But if you put pleasure first, then love goes out of the window. And without this foundation of love, dying every minute to the things that you have accumulated, you cannot live a life of righteous behaviour. This is the foundation. And then we can go into a different dimension altogether. And then meditation has quite a different meaning. Because meditation is not all the fanciful things that are talked about; meditation is emptying the mind of the known and then the mind is young, fresh, innocent, alive, no longer caught in the known but using the known as a tool, not for itself.

Then, in that emptiness, truth has quite a different meaning — it is not a thing of the mind, of the intellect. Now can we, as our time is limited, talk over what has been said; or you can ask questions about something else.

Questioner: I fear death because I love life.

KRISHNAMURTI: I fear death because I love life, that is the question. Comment on it. Do you love life? Do you? There is that soldier in Vietnam, and in Czechoslovakia, the Czechs are suppressed, denied freedom. The man on the battlefield may be killed at any moment, and as for you, going to the office every day of your life for thirty, forty years, think of the boredom of it. Is the thing that you love this life of conflict and misery? Is this love; this hideous mess that we are making? Do not say it is not a mess — you may either have a very comfortable house, with plenty of money, or you may be fighting for a job, competing, struggling, envious — is that what you love? And is love life? Would you hate somebody else? Would you kill some other life? Surely when we say we 'love life', we who say it are all this mess of life which we have formed as pleasure, pain and sorrow. That is how it is.

If the mind could be free of all that, free of it, empty of the known! Most of us are frightened to be alone; we want to be surrounded by people, we are afraid to go out alone and be ourselves, by ourselves, because we might then see ourselves as we are and we are frightened of that. So we surround ourselves with television, telephone, God knows what else, with gods, scriptures, quotations and with an infinite knowledge of things that really do not matter. And that is what we call life and that is what we cling to.

We are naturally frightened of death, not because we love, but because our little ambitions, work and enjoyments come to an end. And that is the sad part of our existence, how frightened we are. Being frightened we invent lovely theories, because we have never said to ourselves that living means dying. To live fully, completely, means dying to all these absurdities. Do you want to ask a question?

Questioner: Is fear ever justified?

KRISHNAMURTI: I do not know quite what this means, do you? Are you saying that self-preservation, physically, is necessary? You do not throw yourself under a bus unless you are a little bit odd. Is fear ever justified? I do not see why it should be justified. Is fear justified, is fear justifiable? To be afraid of something which I have done, which I do not want you to know, there is fear in that. I do not want you to know that I have been a fool or done anything shameful in the past; well, if you know, what of it? Why should I be frightened of what you think? You see I have an image about myself; I have a very righteous, noble, marvellous image about myself. And I do not want you to find out that that image is not as I think it is.

To ask a question is fairly easy. You can throw out any question fairly easily. But to ask the right question is one of the most difficult things. Which does not mean I am preventing you from asking questions. To ask a right question is only possible when you yourself have gone into all this and gone into it very closely. Then when you ask the right question the right answer is there, and you do not even have to ask it. But you must, mustn't you, ask questions, not only about the government, or about your relationship with your wife, your husband and all the rest of it, but also ask questions that are really vital. Like 'what is relationship'? I do not know if you have ever asked it. I am now asking it. What is relationship, not only with your wife and husband but also relationship with your neighbour, with society? What is

42

relationship? Can we go into that? Do you want to go into it? Are you sure it will not be disturbing? I am afraid it is going to be disturbing. Oh! yes it will — I will show you in a minute.

What is relationship? What is the relationship between the stars and yourself — not astrology and all that — just the stars. What is the relationship between you and the cloud in the evening when you see it lit up. What is the relationship between you and your wife, your neighbour. Are you related to your wife? Have you a relationship with your wife, or husband? You have a relationship between that cloud and yourself because you have seen clouds before, you have the memory and the word. And when you say, it is my wife, my husband, what is that relationship? You have an image about your wife and she has an image about you. The husband has built, through many years, an image about her with its pleasure, sex, comfort, annoyance, greed, nagging and all that. And she has an image about you. There is relationship, between the two images, the one you have about her and the other one she has about you. The relationship is between those two images. (No? You are very silent!) And that is what you call relationship. That relationship breeds anxiety, fear, jealousy, the fear of loneliness, the fear of not having a companion. So we establish that relationship legally, it becomes highly respectable. But the relationship is between two images. And when you look at a cloud, at a tree, at the lovely flower, you look at it with the image you have about that flower, cloud or tree.

Now, have we actually a relationship with another? To be related means to be in contact. You may be sexually, physically in contact but that does not constitute a relationship. We are talking of a relationship in which there is no image between you and another. I do not know if you have ever tried it. Do. Have no image about your wife, your husband, your neighbour, or about another; just look, just see, directly,

43

without the image, the symbol, the memory of yesterday, of what she said to you, what you said to her, how she annoyed you and all the rest of it. Stripped of these things there is a possibility of right relationship. Because then everything in that relationship is new; relationship is no longer of the dead past.

Questioner: What does one feel after death?

KRISHNAMURTI: He says, what is your notion, what is your opinion, what do you think happens when you die. Right, Sir? I am afraid you have not followed what I said previously. Sir, when we do not know what living is, we want to know what dying is, and what happens after death. We do not know how to live. When we know how to live, then we know how to die. Then living is dying, otherwise you cannot live. Feeling is something actual, in the immediate; to feel anger, to feel intensely is actual, in the present. But what happens? I feel anger, there is a state of what I call anger — please listen to this — that very word anger is related to the past, you recognise it as anger and give it a name, because you have already experienced it as anger. So when you call it anger you are looking at it with the memory of others angers. Can you look at the present feeling without classifying it, without giving it a name? What happens after death? — that is the question. We can indulge in opinions and say 'this is what I think and that is what you think'. On the one hand there is the intellectual, rational, materialistic opinion, 'that is the end of it, when you die you die'. On the other hand are the so-called spiritual people who have ideas, opinions, beliefs. But neither the materialistic person who says, 'life is lived and when you die you die and that is the end of it', nor the man who says 'there is something extraordinary after death, you are going to live on a cloud or you are going to reincarnate', is giving you the truth; these are only opinions. To find out the truth of the matter you must neither belong to the believers nor to the purely intellectual, rationalistic explainers; the mind must be much more subtle, much more sensitive to find out. Such a mind knows what it means to live by dying every day.

Questioner: What value do you place on social sciences and the understanding of man?

KRISHNAMURTI: Sir, when you have got the whole laboratory inside you, why do you want to 'study man'? Study yourself, the whole human being, you, the whole complexity, beauty, extraordinary sensitivity which is you. Why do you want to study what somebody else says about man? The whole of mankind is you. And you in relationship with another is society. You have created this terrible, ugly world which has become so utterly meaningless, and that is why young people are revolting throughout the world. To me it is such a meaningless life. The society which man has created is the outcome of his own demands, his own urgencies, instincts, ambitions, greed and envy. You think that by reading all the books about man and going in for social study, you are going to understand yourself. Would it not be much more simple to begin with yourself? Look at yourself, without any condemnation or justification, just look, observe the way you talk, the way you argue, discuss, look at all your prejudices, your ambitions — just look. You have the whole history of man right inside yourself, and without knowing yourself first-hand you cannot possibly create a new social order. Not that you must not study society and what other people have written about man and all the rest of it. I, personally, have not studied any of this — you have got the whole thing inside you; look, and you will know a great deal. Sir?

Questioner: Are human beings equal?

KRISHNAMURTI: Are we? You are very clever, I am not. You are highly sensitive and odd. You can think clearly, rationally, beautifully and I am full of prejudices, idiosyncracies, temperament, and these hinder me — you have got a much better job, a bigger car, a bigger house. Your brain is bigger than mine. Is there equality? There may be equality of opportunity. But, why do we compare, why do I say to myself, you have got a much better brain than I have, why? Why am I jealous of you? Through comparison? Obviously we are conditioned to compare from childhood, in school, in business, in the Church where the hierarchical system exists, from the lowly priest to the Pope and so on, but why do we live always comparing? Can the mind cease to compare? Then only would there be a possibility of equality, but not as we are.

Questioner: We have said that living is dying, but what happens to the soul after you die?

KRISHNAMURTI: First: living is dying. Let us look at that. Am I living when I am always living in the past, when the past is always there with its memories, remembrances, is that living? Or when I am living in the future, thinking of what I should be, what I must become, what my position will be or how I was more powerful in the past or will be in the future, am I living? I am living only when there is dying to the past and to the future. Then there is a possibility of living completely in the present, which means living timelessly. And when I live timelessly, is there death? There is this division about soul and spirit and there is the whole Communist world brought up on different ideologies, conditioned differently — they do not believe in spirit and body or spirit and soul. You do because that's how you are conditioned. Is there a soul? Please follow this, do not say it is all nonsense but look at it, examine it. 'The soul', what does that mean? Is it something permanent, to which you can add or subtract but in which there is a quality of permanency; as the Hindus in the Asiatic world say there is 'the Atman'? They are conditioned

46

by that word in the East and you are conditioned by this word 'soul' here. We have to examine it very closely, without fear, questioning it, finding out the truth of the matter, which means being free from conditioning, able to look. Is there in you a permanent state, a permanent quality which you call 'the soul', a permanent spirit? Is there anything permanent? Or does thought give a permanency to a particular thing? You give permanency to the past by thinking about it, the past, your wife, your husband, your house, your whatever it is. And that becomes permanent. Thought gives permanency to anything. I do not know if you ever tried putting a piece of stick on the mantlepiece every day with a flower in front of it. Do this for a while, do it with great devotion, great respect for that stick and see how extraordinarily important that stick becomes. So do our gods and our souls, if we think about them. We are amongst people who are full of soul and spirit — the Hindus with their 'Atman' are most materialistic people, because they worship thought, and thought is always old, it is never new, thought is the response of memory and memory is the dead ashes of yesterday.

When we can look without division at the soul, the spirit, the 'Atman', then we can look at the whole of life without fragmenting it, without breaking it up. Then you will see that there is a beauty that is beyond time and beyond thought.

Questioner: Am I right when I say life is eternal, death does not exist?

KRISHNAMURTI: Does death not exist? You are going to die, one of these days. I may hope you won't but *(laughter)* we are all going to die. And you say that death does not exist. Those people in Vietnam are being killed. Do they say that death does not exist? When my son, brother, sister, wife dies, do I say that death does not exist? I cry, I am lonely, I am miserable; do I say that life is eternal? Life, this life?

47

The life of going to the office every day? Struggle, prejudice, hate, envy, agony, sorrow — do you want that to be eternal? That is all we know, unless we die to all that, not merely in theory but actually put an end to a particular ambition, greed, envy, prejudice, or opinion. If you do this, then you can go very far, then the mind can travel limitlessly. But to live the life we live and call that eternal, merely leads to division, hypocrisy, to an unrealistic state.

Questioner: Man knows he is going to die, so why not put an end to it now, and drop out of society altogether?

KRISHNAMURTI: Are you suggesting that as I am going to die in ten, or fifteen years, I might just as well commit suicide now? Is that it? And can I drop out of society? Can you drop out of society? Do you know what it means to be an outsider in society. By this I mean to have no part, no position, to deny completely and totally the morality of society with its hates and envies, to deny it and be outside it; this would mean, not to hate, not to have prejudice, then you can be an outsider, then you have really dropped out of society. Can you do all that? Sir, dying to the past does not mean committing suicide. If you die to all the stupidities, all the brutality, the arrogance, the pride, the violence, if you do that, you are outside society immediately, psychologically, inwardly, though you may put on a tie and trousers and go to the office to earn money. When you do that you do not belong to this structure.

Questioner: I know how the past works out, but I still continue in the same way.

KRISHNAMURTI: Why? Do you know the past? Do you know what is implied in it? Look, you — not you personally madame, I am speaking impersonally — you are married and you have a husband, you have an image about him and he about you; can you break that image, put an end to that image, immediately? You cannot because you cling to that image; you would be terribly upset if you had no image at all. There is a particular remembrance of a pleasure and it goes on living with you and you are this, you are part of it. And so, you are asking, why it is that though you know the past is obviously in part silly, you go on with it, keeping it. Because there is fear in giving up something, because you are afraid of being lonely, because what you are is the memory of what you have been. Please do listen to this. What you are now is the sum of your memories, and without those memories you are not. What are you? I do not know if you have ever looked at yourself. If you have looked at yourself you will see that you are a bundle of memories, either the memories of the past or of what you may be in the future, projected from the past. That is all that you are, a bundle of words, memories. Sorry to put it so bluntly. And if you say that you won't or will die, or will put away all the past and the future, what are you then? That is the real question — what are you then? To find out what you are then you have to die to the past and to the future. Then you will find out for yourself what it is, in that region where thought doesn't pervade, in that state which is something totally new, instant.

17th September 1968

TALKS AND DISCUSSIONS AT MORCELO,
PUERTO RICO

1

I DO NOT know if you have looked at those hills, dotted with houses, looking very peaceful and rather beautiful. They are not built by the mind, they just happen to be there. And you come here to be told, to be talked at, to be informed, to be persuaded, to be indoctrinated with certain ideas. You want to be persuaded and I am afraid I am not going to do anything of that kind. You have sat here quietly, most unnaturally, before the meeting; somebody must have said, 'Sit quiet, don't talk; this is a serious meeting' and you promptly became quiet; I heard from that house where I am staying, the noise before and after someone said to you, 'You must be quiet' you all became suddenly quiet; this is quite terrible! You want to be told what to do. If you were at all serious, you would naturally be quiet for a little while, without being told to sit quietly, not to applaud, not to do this or do that. If we are natural and serious we instinctively are quiet, faced by those hills and those lovely clouds and open space and blue sky. So please do not be persuaded, talked at, do not wish to be indoctrinated by a new set of ideas. Let us rather talk things over together, like two friends meeting together who are fairly serious and who want to explore the many problems that everyone has. These two friends are not trying to convince each other of any particular point of view or trying to persuade the other that he alone is right. I think that must be clear, that you are free to discuss, free to say what you like, free to observe, not only the hills and the clouds and the blue sky, but also to look at yourselves openly. Otherwise you become hypocritical. You think one thing, feel something

52

else and put on a mask of silence, or of seriousness, or of various types of pretensions, which you do not feel at all.

I would like to go into certain problems and perhaps, if you are also willing, we could explore them together, not only the beauty of the problems but also their complexity and, if it is possible, resolve them. That is why we are here. First of all, let me say: we are so easily persuaded, we so easily obey and conform. That is one of our conditionings imposed on us by society, by the various forms of religious sanctions and social inhibitions, so that we do not know for ourselves what our own problems are nor what are our own feelings, our own clarity of thought. So, to become conscious of what we actually are — not what other people tell us, nor what society or the churches throughout the world have forced man to think along a particular line, but stripping ourselves of all that, denuding ourselves of all the various forms of masks and cloaks that have been put upon us — to become aware of ourselves as we are. That is one of the problems.

You know what I mean by 'aware'? This is an ordinary English word which means to be conscious, to see, to observe everything outside you, these leaves in the wind, the hills, their shape, those shoddy houses, those ugly roads, scarring the hills, just to observe outwardly. Please do this as we go along. And see the colours, the shape of the clouds, the cypress, these two cypresses standing there, and the colour of the foliage, and those blue and yellow butterflies. To observe all this, to observe the people sitting next to you, the coats, whatever the ladies wear, the colours and your reaction to everything. To observe outwardly, to be aware of things externally, and then be aware, if one can, of one's own reaction to all this, why you like this and you do not like that, why you like that particular colour or that particular hill, and the curve and fold of those hills, to observe your reactions. And to find out why you have those reactions,

53

just to observe, not to say, 'This is right or wrong', condemn it, judge it or evaluate it, but just observe your reactions; this is only fairly difficult, because in looking at a tree or those hills one can be aware without any judgment, because they do not personally touch one deeply. But if one looks at oneself and the reactions that one has and observes this, then this is very personal, subjective, very intimate, and so one is not capable of looking quite objectively.

That is one of our problems, to look at the world outside oneself, the politicians, their absurdities, their inanities, their promises, their personal ambitions. To observe everything about you externally and then become aware of yourself and your reactions, and to watch those reactions without any judgment, which is quite arduous. Because you know — when you look at anything, when you look at one of those trees — instinctively you name the tree, don't you? You say, 'That is a cypress, that is an orange tree, that is a banana plant'. The very naming of the objects you see prevents you from looking at them. Do please do it as we are talking — it can be quite fun.

When you name a thing, the very word acts as a distraction from observation. When you use the word 'cypress', you are looking at that tree through the word; so you are not actually looking at the tree. You are looking at that tree through the image that you have built up, and so the image prevents you from looking. In the same way, if you try to look at yourself without the image this is quite strange and deeply disturbing. To look when you are angry, when you are jealous, to look at that feeling without naming it, without putting it into a category. Because when you put it into a category or name it, you are looking at that present state of feeling through the past memory. I don't know if you are following this. So you are actually not looking at the feeling, but you are looking through the memory which has been accumulated when other similar types of feeling arose.

54

So one is never in contact with the tree or with oneself. Is this fairly clear? Because this is important, as you will see presently if you go into it sufficiently deeply. The word, that is the symbol, the description, is not the thing described. The word 'tree' is not the actual tree, and we are likely to be caught in the word. The word prevents us from being in very close contact with the tree. And when we look at ourselves, if we ever do, and if we say, 'That is wrong or right, I have every right to be jealous or envious', these words prevent the actual contact with that feeling, and hence there is a division between the observer and the thing observed. Is this fairly clear? When there is a division between the observer and the observed, that division creates conflict, doesn't it? I am angry; the word anger is already a condemnatory word; so when I say, 'I am angry', I have separated myself from that feeling that I have called anger. There is a division between the observer and the thing observed, which is anger. In that division all other forms of complexities arise. I will show you what I mean. When I say, 'I am angry', I have externalised my anger; so there is a division between the observer and the observed. In that division I condemn anger. In that state of separation there is condemnation or justification and hence conflict; you try to suppress it or to justify it. So the reason of conflict in the human mind is this division between the observer and the observed. And as long as there is conflict, struggle in any form, there is distortion of the mind.

To eliminate distortion or lack of clarity, and hence conflict, to be free of conflict, is to have no division between the observer and the observed. And therefore the mind is capable of looking at things without the distance of time. Is this Greek to you? When one speaks of anyone as a Communist, or a Russian, or of what the Russians have done in Czechoslovakia, and when one gets angry about it or justifies it, when you are the observer and the Russian is the observed, then your particular ideology and his prevent both of you from looking at the other without division.

You know, people have taken L.S.D. and various forms of drugs. I have never taken it because I feel that this would be too immature and childish. But when one has talked to a great many of those who have taken it — this is actually what takes place — the space between the observer and the observed disappears; therefore you see the tree with an astonishing clarity, you see the colour as you have never seen it before, you move in a different dimension chemically. And that is why it is so popular. It gives you an elan, a feeling of tremendous vitality, of observation; what is seen is much more acute, much more intense, colours are incredible. Because there is no conflict, there is no division, there is immediate perception. In the same way, when one can look at oneself with clarity in which there is no division as observer or thinker and the thoughts observed, then you see what actually is, and in that state all conflict disappears.

If one could do this, one would discover for oneself that understanding is not a mental process, is not an intellectual, verbal statement. For the moment that is enough. Shall we discuss that, and then finish with that and go on to something else?

Questioner: Are you identifying yourself with the tree? Are you identifying yourself, subjectively, with anger, and so on.

KRISHNAMURTI: I wonder what we mean by that word identify? To identify oneself with something; that is, to identify myself with India, with the things that happen in India, the poverty, the corruption and the misrule, the appalling state of that poor country, to identify myself with that, as you identify yourself with this country or with Christianity or with whatever it is. Why do we want, first of all, to identify ourselves with anything? This is quite important to discuss. Why do we want to identify ourselves with 'my wife', 'my house', 'my country', 'my God', with anything at all? Why?

First of all, why do I want to identify myself with something? If I do not identify myself with my country, what takes place? I am rather lost, am I not? I feel lonely, I feel an outsider, I am rather afraid, left out, I might lose my job. Therefore I identify myself with my country, which gives me a certain vitality, certain forms of resistance and I feel I belong to the herd. To be alone is very difficult because it invites a great many problems. Now that is the process of identification with something externally, which is really the internal action of identifying oneself with something in order to be secure. That security gives you a certain satisfaction.

Now, when I observe that tree, is it identification with that tree? I am not that tree, obviously, that would be too stupid. I am not that pig that is going by. I observe, I watch, and the space between the observer and the thing observed disappears and I see the thing much more intimately, I see it more, with greater energy, vitality, and intensity. This does not mean that I identify myself with it.

Questioner: Are there degrees of awareness?

KRISHNAMURTI: No. Either you are aware of that tree or you are not aware of it. You see, we give to that word an extraordinary meaning. I am 'aware' of that tree. It is there and I am here. I am aware of that tree only when I give my attention to that tree. But I can look at it casually, or pass it by. Let us be quite simple about these things. I observe the politician, the promises, the vanity, the ambition, the drive for power — he does not believe a thing of what he is talking about; he is out for himself. I observe him, and I see what he is. If I want to be like him, a politician, then I identify myself with him. As most of us are politicians at heart it is quite easy to identify. But if I see the absurdity, the tricks, the inanities of all he says, then there is no relationship.

57

Questioner: Do you become the object?

KRISHNAMURTI: No, you do not become the object. Oh, my God, just think of it!

Questioner: . . . the observer and the thing observed are one.

KRISHNAMURTI: No, Sir, I did not say the observer and the observed are one. I said, when the space disappears between the observer and the observed, a quite different dimension comes into being. I cannot become the tree, I am much too intelligent to become that tree. I think this is quite difficult, Sir, you are quite right to persist in asking that question, because we really do not experience, or come to the feeling that the observer and the observed are one.

Questioner: When I do not justify or condemn, space disappears.

KRISHNAMURTI: Look, Sir, let's put is more directly, then you will, perhaps, see it more closely, intimately. If one is married and has a wife or a husband, then you identify yourself with your wife or with your husband; you identify with that person and what actually takes place? When you identify yourself with your wife do you become her?

Questioner: . . . you become a slave to her.

KRISHNAMURTI: I don't know — you know about this better than I do. *(laughter)* Please do observe a little more, don't say 'I'll become a slave, she dominates me, she is this and she is that'; observe first. Why do I identify myself with my wife or with my husband? What does that mean?

Questioner: It is for security, or pleasure.

KRISHNAMURTI: Consider it for yourself for a minute, you will see it. Go into it for yourself. When I say to myself, 'This is my house', I have identified myself with that house. It is my house; legally I possess it. But why do I give this identifying insistence to it? That is my house. When I say it is my house, the house is more important than myself. The furniture in the house is my furniture. The furniture is much more important than me. So all possessions are much more important than the possessor. And that is what we are. It is my horse and the man who rides it is smaller than the horse itself, both in stature and in his dignity. I don't know if you have observed all this — you must have.

So, our question is, when I identify myself with my wife or with my house, I do it because — I mustn't say it — you tell me why do I do it?

Questioner: We seem more important.

KRISHNAMURTI: No, no. Do look at it a little more. I have just now said, when you possess something, which is a form of identification, the thing you possess becomes far more important. No? Then tell me, please — I may be wrong. I may be wrong, Madame. When we identify with goodness, which he may have or she may have, that identification is the recognition of my lack of it and I want it. Is that it? Then why do I not identify myself with her when she nags me? You identify yourself with something which you call good and you do not identify yourself with what you call bad.

Questioner: I try to fix that feeling . . .

KRISHNAMURTI: Sir, look, all this implies non-freedom, doesn't it? 'My family', 'my house', 'my country', 'my God', 'my belief' — obviously identifying myself with something is the state of being a prisoner, it does not give you freedom to look. When the Russian identifies himself with his government, he cannot possibly look at what he is doing in Czechoslovakia. And I cannot, if I identify myself with my wife, see what she is. Which means that I am not free. It is not a case of not being free *from* her, but that there is no state of freedom in me.

59

Questioner: Inaudible.

KRISHNAMURTI: Of course, Sir, that is implied. So, from that you can see that only in freedom can you look.

Questioner: What then is the reality of time and space?

KRISHNAMURTI: Some philosophers say that that is a thing of the mind. Perhaps Sir, we can take that up after we have finished this, after we have finished this question of observing.

Questioner: What impedes us from having this freedom?

KRISHNAMURTI: I think nothing impedes you except yourself.

Questioner: ... call things by their names ...

KRISHNAMURTI: That is just it, Sir, there is an automatic reaction to things by calling them immediately by name. How can we prevent it? You cannot. You have to realize how you are conditioned, when you meet a black man or pink. Whatever it is, your reaction is immediate, because your culture, your education, has so deeply conditioned you. You know, in India, this conditioning has been going on, not for two thousand years as here, but for some ten thousand years. And the conditioning is tremendous, centuries old. To be free of it is not a question of time; we can cut through it, finish with it; and when we see its absurdity, we end it.

Questioner: Can we go into the question of time here?

KRISHNAMURTI: The question is, that we may cut it immediately, but does this last? Now, can we go into this question of time which you previously raised, time and space? Now, he said, I can cut it immediately but it does not last. The 'lasting' is a question of time. Time is duration, isn't it? That is, I can be instantly non-angry, but this state does not last, I may be angry again next minute. So, one has to find out what time is; not what some philosophers say — because I

60

do not know what they say, I do not read books at all, fortunately for me. One can see what time is. What is time? There is time by the watch, chronological time, the time it takes to go from here to a house; time involves the covering of that space between here and your house. The house is a fixed object — please listen to this carefully — the house is a fixed object and the time that it takes to cover that distance is measurable. So there is time according to the watch. That is clear. There was time as yesterday, today and tomorrow, which again is part of chronological time; yesterday I was in London, today I am here, tomorrow I am in New York. Again, this covers distance through time by the watch. That is clear. I am not a philosopher therefore please forgive me. (*Laughter*) Is there any other time?

Questioner: The time we spend in life?

KRISHNAMURTI: That is, what? The days you spend in living? The time, growing old, dying, covering a space and ending? Please, I am asking something, do listen to it. Is there any other time except chronological time.

Questioner: Psychological time.

KRISHNAMURTI: There is a time which is called psychological. So there are two times, the time of yesterday, today and tomorrow, the distance, the time you take between here and your house; that is one kind of time. It takes time to learn a language, collecting a lot of words, memorising them; that will take time. Learning a technique, learning a craft, learning a skill — all that implies time — chronological time. Then there is psychological time, the time that mind has invented. The mind that says, I will be the President, tomorrow I will be good, I will achieve, I will become successful, I will be more prosperous, I will attain perfection, I will become the Commissar, I will be this, I will be that. There, time is between the goal and the present state. That goal which I have set myself to achieve, will take time — I must struggle, I must drive, I must be ambitious, I must be brutal, I must push everybody aside. These are all projections of the mind and what it wants to achieve; they create psychological time. So we have these two kinds of time, chronological time and psychological time.

Questioner: Is there any difference? I do become the President or I do learn Italian and this say takes six months or six years.

KRISHNAMURTI: Yes, is does take time. I recognise these two states, the chronological and the psychological. But is psychological time true or is it an illusion? You haven't understood, Sir? I am asking myself, does psychological time exist at all?

Questioner: Inaudible.

KRISHNAMURTI: Yes, Sir, I understand, but we have to go into it very deeply, we must go very slowly. Don't let us assert anything. Do not say, it is an illusion, it is not an illusion, it is like this or like that, do not let us fall into that absurdity. Here are two facts, one, I am this, the other that I want to be that, whether it is a big thing or a little thing. And that also implies space and time. And the other is getting from here to the house, distance to cover, involving time. I say to myself, both seem to be true, true in the sense that I have a goal, I want to be powerful, I want to be rich, I want to be famous, and I drive towards that. To become famous takes time, because the image which I have created of fame is there in the distance and I must cover it, through time, because I am not that image now, but I will be in the future. I am not at the house now. I am here. It will take time. And now I want to be famous. Psychologically, that is my projection, the image which I have created of fame. You see that, there it is. I have projected it, it is my image because I have compared other famous people and I want to be like them.

And that implies struggle, competitiveness and ruthlessness. It is an actual thing I want, do I not? I want that and I struggle to get it. I do not question why I have created that image. I do not question what is involved in arriving at that image. I just say, 'I must be that image'. So in this there is a great deal of conflict, pain, suffering, and brutality. And that is my conditioning, because people have told me from childhood that I must be this, I must pass my exams, I must be a great man, I must be a business man, a lawyer, a professor, whatever it is.

So I have created that image and I have not found out why I have done so. If I see the absurdity of that image, if I see the futility, the pain, the agony, the anxiety, everything that is involved in it, I do not create the image, therefore I abolish it.

Questioner: What is wrong with learning Italian in time?

KRISHNAMURTI: No, please, do not mix up the two, please keep it . . .

Questioner: Two psychological states, I am nobody and to morrow I will be somebody.

KRISHNAMURTI: I am nobody and tomorrow I will be somebody. The 'tomorrow' is there in my mind. I am waiting for tomorrow to happen. So there is time (or I think there is). I will be famous. The words 'will be' are in the future. So, I ask myself, is there a tomorrow at all? Tomorrow exists only when I want to be something.

Questioner: Can I be free of psychological time?

KRISHNAMURTI: I am showing it to you, Sir. Can man be free from psychological time? Find out for yourself, Sirs; you can see it. If I want to be famous, I cannot be free from time. If I say, I am nobody, and I want to be somebody, I am a slave to time. Now I am nobody, why should I be someone? — I am nobody.

63

Questioner: Inaudible.

KRISHNAMURTI: No, the somebody has a bigger car, a bigger house. Don't let's mix up words. I am nobody, but I want to be somebody. There is in this the whole process of time. If I do not want to be anybody, is there psychological time? I am what I am. But if I want to change myself into something, then time begins. But I must change, I cannot remain as I am. Are you following all this?

Look, I am nobody. Please follow this step by step. I am nobody and I want to be somebody. In that is involved time, pain and the rest. The demand for being somebody, for change from being nobody, that kind of change I discard as it is absurd, unintelligent, immature. So I say, I am nobody. If I remain as nobody, there is nothing. I am nobody, there is nothing in me. But that quality must also change. Those poor chaps in those huts, (I do not know how you can stand those huts around here!) — that poor chap in that hut — he is nobody. He cannot become anybody because he is uneducated, he is this and he is that. But he also wants to become somebody because he sees the house next door is a bigger house. So the wanting to be somebody is through comparison. We all look at this through comparison. Now, can the mind eliminate all comparison? Then I will not say, 'I am nobody'.

Why should I project? I want to learn Italian and I will learn it. It will take time and I will work at it. I have to be in New York on the 23rd of this month. I will plan, I will buy a ticket. There is no projection, there is no image, I have to do the practical things that will get me there. But I might say to myself: 'I am going to New York and it will be much more exciting than living here and all the rest of it'. Now is it possible for the mind not to compare and therefore — but you do not see the beauty of it — and therefore have no time at all. Am I answering your question, Sir?

Questioner: Inaudible.

KRISHNAMURTI: I said, when you say you are nobody, you have already compared yourself with someone who is somebody. If you eliminate all comparison you will have completely changed. I am still living in that filthy little hut. So the man who lives in that filthy little house, if he comes to this point of saying, 'All comparison has come to an end', will be out of that house.

Questioner: How?

KRISHNAMURTI: He will work more intelligently.

Questioner: Why would he work if he had not seen the bigger house next door?

KRISHNAMURTI: That is just it. If there is no comparison, what takes place? This is the first question; what actually takes place when you do not compare?

Questioner: You are not blocking yourself any more.

KRISHNAMURTI: He says, you are not blocking yourself any more. Look, let us begin. Why do you compare? You begin at school, the teacher tells you you are not doing well, not as well as the other boy. The whole process of examinations, marks and all that is comparison. From childhood you are conditioned to compare, compare the little house with the big house; always comparing. That is your conditioning. And it brings about a series of struggles, of success and failure, of miseries, which society and yourself have imposed. That is your conditioning. You see the poor boy becoming President. That is a tremendous advertisement; and you say, 'What a marvellous competitive society this is!' That is our conditioning. And we maintain it because sometimes it is profitable, sometimes it is painful, but it is incurable. We never question why we compare. Please question it now and find out. Why do you compare?

65

Questioner: One feels insufficient.

KRISHNAMURTI: Take this up — when you feel insufficient you compare. But how do you know that you are insufficient, if you do not compare? Please go into this. Do we compare because we are insufficient? Do we compare because it is part of our conditioning? Every newspaper says, look, so and so is so powerful and you are nobody. So we accept comparison as the norm, as the inevitable process of existence. I do not. Why should I compare? If I do not compare, am I a nobody? I only compare with something superior and therefore I feel inferior. And if I have no comparison I am ...

Questioner: Unique?

KRISHNAMURTI: No, it has nothing to do with uniqueness. How do I know I am unique? Because I have compared with those people who are not unique? How do I know? To use this word — please Sir, stick to this, it is very interesting to go into it. Look, I compare two pieces of cloth when I buy a coat. Black and White. I compare. I compare this country, saying, 'It is very hot here'; but I can say that this is a very hot country without comparing. If I compare this country with a cooler country, I resist this heat, and then this heat becomes intolerable. Can one eliminate comparison, psychologically, and keep away from comparison with regard to big house, little house, bigger carpet ...

Questioner: What is the mechanism of comparison?

KRISHNAMURTI: You can see why we compare because, for one thing, we are conditioned, and also through comparison we think we are living. It is part of our struggle; by comparing we feel that we are acting. We say, if I do not compare, if I do not become like Mr. Smith, my God, what shall I be? So comparison is the system in which we have been born, which either says, 'You must be an executive, you must

66

we (I) am conditioned that
to compare or I think that living — Illusion
through it I am living

have millions', or on the other hand, 'You must be a saint and have nothing'.

Questioner: Can one be satisfied with what one is and not be concerned with the neighbour?

KRISHNAMURTI: Are you really concerned with the neighbour? That neighbour down below? Are you? Obviously not. And you are not satisfied with what you are. The moment you use the word 'satisfied' and 'not satisfied' there is comparison. Obviously. So, you eliminate altogether words like 'better', 'the more'. So you see, time, psychological time exists only when there is a state of comparison and that includes dissatisfaction, feeling of inferiority, feeling that you must achieve, that you must be — all that is implied in comparison. And when you say, 'I am nobody', that word is a comparative word, otherwise you would not use that word. So time, psychological time exists when there is this comparative mind, the mind that measures psychologically. Now, can I, can the mind exist without measuring — exist, live, not just go to sleep — be tremendously active, alive to its fullest depth? That is only possible when there is no comparison.

Psychological time exists only when there is comparison, when there is a distance to be covered between 'what is' and 'what should be', which is the desire to become somebody or nobody, all that involves psychological time and the distance to be covered. So one says, is there a tomorrow, psychologically? And this you will not be able to answer. Is there tomorrow — 'tomorrow' having come into being because I have had a moment of complete freedom, a complete feeling of something, and it has gone. I would like to keep it, to make it last. Making it last is a form of greed. We struggle to achieve that thing again. All this is implied in psychological time. When you have some experience of joy, of pleasure or whatever it is, live it completely and do not demand that it should endure, because then you are caught in time.

So, is there tomorrow? That is, tomorrow is ahead and I have had a feeling today of great happiness and want to know if it will last. How can I keep it so that it will always last? Memory of that pleasure makes you want that memory to continue and if it continues, you prevent further experience altogether. It is fairly simple, this.

Questioner: (In Spanish)

KRISHNAMURTI: If you speak Spanish slowly I can understand; I think you have said: 'How can I understand resistance'? Again, what do you mean by that word 'resist'?

Questioner: (In French)

KRISHNAMURTI: First, let us look at that word, what it means, not what you feel or I think or somebody else thinks — first, see what the word 'to resist' means. To resist involves time; to oppose, to resist, to put a barrier, to put it away from you. To resist — I resist the rain, I resist the sunshine, I do not like it, I resist temptation, I resist; I want a bigger house and I say 'How stupid, I am not going to have it'. So I resist, rebel against something which I want, or don't want. Why should I resist at all? Please put this to yourself: 'Why should I resist'? That has been all my life, I have resisted this and I have accepted that, I don't like this and I like that. So I have built a wall of resistance all round myself, obviously. I don't want to go into this too deeply but let's touch on it briefly; I have resisted everything, I have resisted this and that, so I have built a wall around myself. And the wall is the 'me' and the 'me' is the very essence of resistance. So why do I resist?

I resist. I resist temptation. But what I want to know is why there is resistance at all. Why can't I look at something and understand it — why should I resist it? Do look at it, Sir — I resist only something which I don't understand. I say 'Ecco' — I understand that. To maintain a particular

68

state I resist; I was happy yesterday and I resist anything that will prevent me having that experience again. If I could look at everything with clarity, then there would be no resistance, would there? If I look with clarity at the process of the modern, or of the old world, there everybody wants to be somebody, or nobody, look at it, see everything involved in it, the pain, ugliness, brutality, failure, and bitterness of it all, if I understand it all then it is finished — I will no longer resist anything. Anything else, Sirs?

Questioner: We go from one conditioning to another . . .

KRISHNAMURTI: Yes, is not freedom from one conditioning a form of another conditioning? If I understand or am aware choicelessly of my conditioning, would I fall into another? Then I recognise all conditioning, whether it is from this or from that, recognise it, understand it, look at it, go into it. You know, it is like those people who go from one religion to another, from one sect to another, and they think they are becoming tremendously religious. But that is childish.

14th September 1968

IT SEEMS TO me that one of our major problems is how to bring about total and complete action in our life. Our life as it is, is broken up, fragmentary; we are scientists, engineers and so on. We are specialised technologically, and inwardly also we are in different fragments — we are at moments pacifists, at moments aggressive and brutal and at other times we are tender and quiet. So there is in our life, both outwardly and inwardly a constant cleavage, a constant fragmentation, the breaking up of a life, which being contradictory, brings about confusion and pain. We are drawn by one desire, by one pleasure opposed to another pleasure and so on. This I think is recognizable, one can observe this if one is sufficiently interested; it is there, this fragmentation is going on. Each fragment has its own activity, its own action. Hence our life is fragmentary, a destructive and contradictory existence. I think that is fairly clear, isn't it?

One asks oneself if it is at all possible, not theoretically but actually, to lead a life that is always whole, that is always non-fragmentary. So that whatever the activity is, it is complete, not broken up, contradictory, opposing or resisting. I think that is an inevitable question when one observes the fragmentation that goes on in one's life. Now can we proceed from there?

I hope the question is clear to you. One is pulled in different directions and there is a great sense of frustration, a deep sense of inadequacy, in dealing with the totality of life. For instance, one is a politician of a certain party, or a Communist, a socialist, a Catholic, a Protestant, each with its own particular beliefs. And one asks if one can live a life that is completely whole, (I do not like to use the word integrated because it is not an integration at all) a life that is non-fragmentary, that is always flowering without a break, without fragmentation, without cleavage. If this is clear, then the next question is: what can one do? One's life is broken up between office, home, ambition and all the rest of it. It is broken up. Then, can one lead a life that is so complete that there is no contradiction at all in it? Now what do you say to that question? I am speaking of a life that is not a spiritual life nor a mundane life, not a religious life nor a secular life. There is a challenge. And how do you respond to it? No answer?

Questioner: I don't quite understand.

KRISHNAMURTI: No, sir, don't use a word, one word doesn't cover everything. One must go into it a little more deeply, not just use a universal blanket that will cover up everything. What makes for contradiction? I see a life broken up. I am kind at home and brutal in the office; I am divided. First of all, one has to find out what is the cause of this fragmentation. Why I am one thing at one time and at another completely different. Why? What is the cause of this fragmentation, this division? How do you find out? What process do you use — we are talking like friends, there is no teacher and disciple here at all — one has to be both a teacher and a disciple to oneself, so there is no teacher and disciple here or a sense of authority. So, how does one find out what is the cause of this fragmentation?

Questioner: Inaudible.

KRISHNAMURTI: No, you are going back to yesterday, forget yesterday.

Questioner: We want first of all your opinion . . .

71

KRISHNAMURTI: The gentleman says he wants to know my opinion first. We are not dealing with opinions. You can say, it's your opinion, my opinion and his opinion, but opinions have no value at all — you can leave that to the politicians and to the intellectuals. But here is a thing that you have to find out. *You* have to find out; it is not I who have to find out and tell you what to do. We can go into it together, explore it, but if you say, I'll wait till you tell me, then there is no fun in it.

Questioner: How can I know the fragmentation if I do not know the whole?

KRISHNAMURTI: I am fragmented, there it is — I go to the office, there I am brutal, I am envious, I am vicious, I am competitive. And at home I am very quiet, very gentle, dominated by my wife or I dominate her and so on. There is a fragmentation. We are asking, why is there such a fragmentation, what is the cause of it?

Questioner: We live in opposites, but why?

KRISHNAMURTI: The questioner says, we live in opposites, but why?

Questioner: There is no love.

KRISHNAMURTI: That is not an answer — is it? — when you say 'there is no love'. We are examining the question and if you say, 'there is no love', then you cannot go any further. We are examining it, exploring why we live in duality, why we constantly swing from one point of view to the other between opposites; why we live in a corridor of opposites, why.

Questioner: We have no control over circumstances in our life.

KRISHNAMURTI: That is true but that is not the question.

72

Questioner: We are looking for satisfaction.

KRISHNAMURTI: Oh no, not looking for satisfaction; you see — now, may I suggest something? Before you give an opinion, as you are now doing, find out why one lives in this condition; what is the cause of it.

Questioner: There is duality.

KRISHNAMURTI: Duality — but why? You are giving a new set of responses, but you really do not know. Please do not guess, because then we shall be lost. Do not guess, don't try several things out to find out if it is so. When you say 'I really do not know' as it has been suggested, you admit that you do not know what the cause of it is. That is the only right approach, isn't it? I really do not know. That would be a fair statement; I really do not know why I live in duality. Now, I do not know, but how am I going to find out?

Questioner: (Various indistinct interjections by questioners.)

KRISHNAMURTI: Do you give up this game? When you do not know, what do you do? Let us proceed from there. I do not know, you do not know why we live in this contradiction. When you say, I do not know, how do you then proceed? How do you find out? Wait, please go slowly. How do you find out — by thinking? Now, what do you mean by thinking? Analyse the problem? Wait, wait. Analyse the problem. The problem involves division, contradiction, fragmentation. I have analysed it and I see my life split up. And I am asking why. And you say, think about it, use thought to find out. Thought! Now, what is thought? Before I say I will use it, I must go into the question of what thought is. Thought obviously is the response of memory. No?

Questioner: One of the causes is our fear.

KRISHNAMURTI: No, sir; you make a statement and block yourself. You are not prepared to examine, to explore, so do

73

not make a statement. A gentleman said there that the instrument of investigation, of analysis, is thought. But will thought uncover it? We think it may uncover it, and therefore say, 'I will find out what thought is'. Now what is thinking? Please do not just guess. Do look at it. What is thinking? I ask you where you live and your response to that question is immediate because you know, you are familiar with the street, with the number and so on; you answer the question instantly. There is no interval between the question and the answer. Now if I ask you a slightly more complex question, there is an interval between the question and the answer. What takes place in that interval?

Questioner: Mental activity, that is, thinking.

KRISHNAMURTI: What takes place there? I ask you the distance from here to New York and you do not know or you have been told but you have forgotten it. So what takes place? I do not know, therefore I begin to look into my memory; thought begins to examine the store of memory. I have read somewhere that it is so many miles from here to New York and I ask people and at last I answer that question. It is so many miles. That is what we call thinking. The question is put, there is an interval before the response, in that interval there is a great deal of enquiry, analysis, asking, expecting, waiting. That is what we call mental activity, reasonable or unreasonable. Now when I ask you a question to which you do not know the answer, what takes place then? You cannot appeal to your memory. You cannot say 'I will find out'. Nobody can answer you. So what takes place?

Questioner: You use your imagination or intuition.

KRISHNAMURTI: Imagination? I cannot imagine something which I do not know. Intuition? That might be guess-work. Follow this step by step; you will find out for yourself. I ask a familiar question and you answer it immediately. I ask

74

another question which is a little more complex, a little more difficult, and you take time over it. In that interval of time you are cogitating, thinking, watching, looking, asking. Now, I am asking you what is the cause of this fragmentation about which we were speaking and you do not know. If you knew, it would be according to your memory, wouldn't it? So, 'I really do not know' would be the most honest answer. I really do not know.

Wait a minute, have patience. If I do not know, what do I do? I cannot go to a professor and ask this question. I cannot look into any book. No book will tell me. And I have to find out because it is a very serious question, because if I can change this whole activity of life which is fragmented, I will live differently, entirely differently. So I, as a human being, have to find out. I cannot depend on anybody. It may be guess-work, it may be wrong, it may be false. But I must find out. Now, how do I proceed to find out?

Questioner: We compare.

KRISHNAMURTI: No, sir, that is still thought.

Questioner: A man's life may stop being fragmentory.

KRISHNAMURTI: That is too simple, sir; it may stop, but it never will.

Questioner: I don't know where I am going.

KRISHNAMURTI: So when you say you do not know, is thought still in operation? I do not know — I want to find out and there is nobody who is going to tell me. And I will not let anybody tell me. Because they may be utterly wrong — they generally are. I have no faith in anybody because all of the people whom I have trusted, the priests, the philosophers, the politician, the Communist, the socialist have all failed. So I must find out and what I discover must be true under all circumstances. Wait, listen to me please, do listen.

So I am not going to ask anybody and I do not know why I live a life which is so broken up. And I want to find out. How are you going to find out? I am asking how you are going to find it?

Questioner: (Inaudible)

KRISHNAMURTI: Madam, we are not asking how to look at ourselves, but what we are asking is when you do not know the answer to a very important, vital question, what do you do? Do you give up? Wait; you do not give up, do you? When you are hungry, tremendously hungry, you do not give up. And if this question is as serious as hunger, do you give up and say 'I don't know, I don't care'? It is a tremendously vital question.

Questioner: That sounds very materialistic.

KRISHNAMURTI: Materialistic? No, sir, it is not materialistic; I do not know what you mean by materialistic.

Questioner: My brain is the storehouse of memory.

KRISHNAMURTI: Yes, sir, my brain is the storehouse of memory, of experience, of knowledge but that brain has no answer now. I used that brain before to find the ordinary answer, depending on people and so on, but now it fails. So what am I to do? I have been a Communist, a socialist, a religious man, I have been through every type of fragmentation, one after the other, and I say 'What a stupid way of living'! And yet I go on. I want to find out why. I live a life of fragmentation, in bits and pieces and I cannot ask anybody for an answer. I want to find out. What am I to do?

Questioner: You have to meditate.

KRISHNAMURTI: Wait, sir, we are doing that now, we are doing that. We are meditating now, but you refuse to — I do not use that word.

Questioner: We must go in for self-examination. There is lack of harmony in ourselves.

KRISHNAMURTI: No, madam, we have examined ourselves. That 'lack of harmony in ourselves' is not an answer.

Questioner: (Inaudible)

KRISHNAMURTI: No — you are quoting — please do not.

Questioner: We look for divine inspiration.

KRISHNAMURTI: 'Look for divine inspiration' — wait a minute, sir. Suppose I am a non-believer, and I cannot look. Inspiration! You believe in it because you are conditioned, as a Catholic, as a Hindu or a Buddhist and you look according to your conditioning for that inspiration. We are meditating — please follow this slowly — we are meditating, we are very carefully going into this step by step. You are going to find out. I did not really want to use that word 'meditation', as that is a very difficult word; it means something entirely different from what is usually called by that name. But we will use it for the time being in order to understand this immense problem, sir.

Questioner: I am living with it now.

KRISHNAMURTI: You are living with it now. *(laughter)* You see, one of our difficulties is, you are not used to this kind of examination; you are learning to observe. We want to observe how in our life, everything is fragmented. That is very clear. We have different desires pulling one against the other, different pleasures; we are peaceful at one moment, war-mongering the other, aggressive then kind, and so on. We believe, we do not believe; despair and hope alternate, we live in contradictions and opposites. I say to myself, why? Why do I live this way? Just listen to me for two minutes, sir. Why do I live this way? Madame, would you just give

77

me two minutes? Let me talk for a little and then you can put your questions.

My life and yours are in fragmentation, broken up. We lead a dual kind of life, say one thing, do another, think one thing and say something else. This contradiction, this duality, that is the life one leads. And I am asking why? Why is life so fragmented? And I cannot ask anybody, because their own life is fragmented. They will guess, they will say, it is your conditioning, it is God, it is society, it is this, it is that. So I cannot ask anybody, therefore I have to find out for myself. And what I find out must be true. It must be absolutely true. Now, how do I find out? I really do not know and I have used thought as an instrument to find out all my life. All my life I have used thought, asking, using memory, knowledge and experience — I have used all these to find out. And here I cannot rely on my knowledge because knowledge says, 'I do not know'. Knowledge says, 'that is the individual way of life'. So there is no dependence on knowledge, on experience or on what people say. Therefore I discard all that, completely. And now what am I to do, how am I going to find out what is truth?

How do I now look on this fragmentation. You understand my question? I do not know, but there must be a right answer. What has happened to my mind now? Let me put the question differently. Probably most of you are conditioned to believe in God, what you call being spiritual. And if you really want to find out — not repeat, not have faith, not say 'it is so' — if you really want to find out if there is such a thing as God, you have to discard all beliefs, haven't you? You must be free of all beliefs to find out. You must be free of fear to enquire, to give your life to find out. Now, in the same way, I want to find out the truth of this matter. What is the state of my mind that has discarded authority, that has given up asking somebody else to tell me, that has discarded knowledge, because knowledge is always of the past? This

78

is a question that must be answered now, not according to the terms of the past, but now. Therefore I must discard knowledge as a means of enquiry. And I must not be frightened; there may be no answer at all, contradiction may be the way of life. I must not be frightened, there must be no fear of any authority, including that of my experience, my knowledge or other people's knowledge — there must be complete freedom for enquiry. Now, what is the state of mind that is free to look? You understand my question? Don't answer me please.

Questioner: Please repeat the question!

KRISHNAMURTI: I cannot repeat the question but I will put it differently. Look, sir, I have lived a life depending on others, on what people say, what the Church has taught me or what the authorities have told me about this and that, and here is a problem which no authority can answer. And I do not trust any authority, because they have led me up the wrong path. So, what is the state of my mind that has refused to accept what other people say; what are my own feelings, my own intuitions? — because these may also be very deceptive. I have no fear, because I do not care if I have to suffer; this is my way of life, that is, I accept it. So I am not afraid, and I say to myself 'what is the state of the mind which is not afraid, which is not accepting any authority, or looking for some divine superior intuitive answer?' I refuse to do all that. I say to myself 'I have done with that'. Then what is the state of my mind that has done this?

Questioner: It is completely denuded of all influence, conditioning, fear.

KRISHNAMURTI: Now, wait, if it is that, then there is not any contradiction. When there is no duality then there is the answer. Please do not answer me, look at it. You are then living in a different dimension. Therefore to find out anything fundamental, like the answer to this issue, is not to be afraid, not to ask, not to say 'Please tell me what is the answer', not to be frightened, whatever it is. Now can you do it? If you cannot, you must lead the dualistic life, a contradictory, painful, sorrowing life.

You see unfortunately we do not like to be put into a corner like this. You want to find an easy outlet, an easy way of escape. So the question is; why do you live this way, knowing very clearly now what is involved in the dualistic life, and knowing also that one can completely get out of it, by not being afraid; what will you do? Just go on playing as before?

You know what meditation is? I am afraid you do not. Or you have read about it in some book or other, and that is too bad. Real meditation exists and is what we are talking about. To empty the mind of the known, as fear. Do you want to talk about something else?

Questioner: You mentioned yesterday the question of Russia and Czechoslovakia. Do you not think if the super powers do not stop hating each other, competing with each other for world markets and all the rest of it, we are going to be destroyed?

KRISHNAMURTI: Now, how are you going to stop Russia or America from preparing for defence, as they call it? Would you tell me? Russia, with its three million men in arms, and America with so many millions, how are you going to prevent it? There is tremendous vested interest, isn't there, in the army, in the officers, at the Pentagon, at the Kremlin, tremendous vested personal interest. Now, do you mean to say the admiral or the general is going to give everything up? Because there must be peace in the world? What do you say? What will you do? Please, pursue this question to the very end, if you are not too tired. How are we going to prevent this division that is going on in the world — two great powers, super powers, with their spheres of influence, with their vested interest — think what they have invested in armaments! What are they going to do? This division will exist as long as the citizens of those countries and other countries feel patriotic, nationalistic. No?

Questioner: (Inaudible)

KRISHNAMURTI: If you hate the Russians and love the Americans, if you feel nationalistic saying 'my country first and everybody else second', and if you cannot depend on these great powers to end wars, it must begin with us. No? The minority, the few who feel things very strongly, the minority has always moved forward and brought about a different position in the world. But we are not willing to be in the minority. Which means this thing is very complex, it is not just 'there you are', it is very complex. Now, the speaker personally is not a Hindu — that is a terrible, ugly thing, to call oneself a Hindu. But here is a passport, Indian passport, otherwise you could not travel. And if you use the aeroplane, the railway, the stamp, you are supporting war. No? What do you say — aren't you?

If you pay taxes, then you support the war. So what are you to do? Are you not going to pay taxes? Not travel? Not buy stamps? I know people who have done this, who will not travel, so they limit their activities to a very small field, and it is absurd not to pay taxes because you will go to prison if you do not. It would be absurd not to buy a stamp, because you could not write letters. And so on. But do not let us give importance or emphasis to secondary issues, like the stamp or the tax and such little things but let us get involved in the primary issue which is not to be nationalistic, not to be patriotic, respond to colour prejudice or any of the rest of the mess one indulges in. And that requires a great deal of intelligence. To decide not to be nationalistic means nothing, but to consider this whole problem one has to be

81

very intelligent which means very sensitive to all the issues. Any more questions?

Questioner: What is your position, what is my position if the country or the army calls me, drafts me or conscripts me to join the army and I do not believe in killing.

KRISHNAMURTI: Is this a trap for me? *(laughter)* Wait, wait. If you are really serious, that you do not want to kill, not just saying, 'I do not want to kill', but really meaning not to kill, you have to live peacefully, haven't you? Do not kill animals. For your food, do not kill. Do not kill by words; do not say, 'he is an awful man, he is a stupid man'. You are killing, verbally, you are killing with words, with gestures, with thought, in the office, in the Church, everywhere you are killing. So if you really do not want to kill, you have to begin a life which is really peaceful. But you won't. You see, you listen to all this. You give lip-service or listen quietly but you go back home, you do the whole thing all over again. Therefore you are supporting war.

Questioner: Very many young people object in America and I am sure they object in Russia.

KRISHNAMURTI: I do not know if you read that article by one of the top scientists in Russia, who is objecting to a great many things that the Soviet Government is doing. This is going on right through the world, and it is not just Russia and America. In India, public opinion demands that you must be a nationalist, and when I talk in India about not being a nationalist they say, 'go and talk in other countries, not here'. Are you tired . . . ? You are too eager to say no. Because what we are discussing is very serious and a mind that is serious cannot just say, 'I am not tired', it has to be tremendously active. The question is, you are not aware, you are not conscious of your fragmentary life. And you can only be aware of it if you become very attentive to your life, to the way you live. And, what is attention? That is the question, Sir, isn't it? Does this interest you? But please do it — don't just say yes and drop it. What does attention mean? To attend. When is it an intellectual process? What do we mean by attention, not the soldier's attention, but what do we mean by attention, to attend. When do you attend? You attend only when you give your mind and your heart and your whole being to something. When I listen to the cry of that child, if there is any form of resistance to that child crying, to the noise, I am inattentive. Don't you see? When one gives attention, the implication is that your nerves, your body, your heart and your whole mind give attention to something of which you want to be aware. And we never do. I do not know if you have ever done this, given attention, let us say, to that tree. This means what? To give attention means, not to describe the tree, not to be caught in the verbal statement about that tree. If I use the word 'cypress' it is a distraction, isn't it? This prevents me from giving my complete attention to looking at the tree. To attend means, to attend intellectually, emotionally, with your nerves, with your eyes, with your ears, with everything that you have. To attend, to look. And we have never done it because we live in fragments. Only when there is a tremendous crisis in our life, then we may perhaps give attention for a few seconds, and then go away from it, escape from it.

Now, if one is at all serious and one wants to find out if there is a reality, God or what you like to call it, one does not look to any authority, to any priest, to any belief; all that is too childish and immature. One has to give all one's attention to find out. One cannot give attention, completely, if one is afraid of losing one's job, in finding out. One cannot give complete attention to find out the truth of this matter if one relies on some belief, on some conditioning, or what people have said. One has to discard that. One cannot belong to any society, to any group, to any culture to find out. Which means one must be completely alone, inwardly alone. Then one will find out. But if one is not attentive in that deep, profound sense of that word, one cannot possibly come upon that reality. Yes, Sir?

Questioner: Have you come to that state of mind?

KRISHNAMURTI: Are you, the questioner says, in that state of mind? First of all, why do you ask that question? I am not avoiding it, Sir, I will reply to it. Why do you ask that question?

Questioner: Because the question is difficult.

KRISHNAMURTI: I am asking that, the gentleman says, because it is rather difficult. I do not think it is difficult. Wait, Sir, I am answering. First of all, if I say 'yes', it will have no value, will it? To you it will have no value because what is the good of my saying 'yes'. Then you accept it or reject it. You might say, 'poor chap, he is a little bit crazy', or you will say, 'he is serious, it might be true'. So my statement that there is such a state has no value for another. What has value is whether you can find it; you, not somebody else. And when you say it is difficult, when you use the very word difficult, you are preventing yourself. Sir, if we accept life as it is, with the misery, with the sorrow, with the conflict, with so much agony, if we accept it, then there is no answer, that is the way of life. If we do not accept it, if we refuse to belong to the herd, to the group, then we begin to live differently. It is absolutely necessary to find out — to live quite differently.

Questioner: Can you develop attention by practice?

KRISHNAMURTI: Practice means repetition, doing something over and over again. Is that attention? That is mechanical, isn't it? So, there are two things involved, if you are serious; there is inattention and attention. Now, most of us are inattentive. And we say it is important not to be inattentive, but to be attentive. Then you want to begin to practice it. But if you say: 'look, I am going to be aware, attentive to my in-attention', do you know what that means, to be inattentive? We accept things as they are, our life, the way we live, the ugly emotions, all 'that is', actually. And to become attentive is to be aware of the inattention, not to try to become attentive, because that involves conflict, struggle and therefore when you practice attention it becomes mechanical. And that ceases to be attention. Whereas if one is attentive, aware of inattention, then out of that flowers attention. (Is that enough for this morning?) You see, I have been working, the speaker has been working, this talk has now lasted for an hour and a half, he has worked. But you haven't worked, you have just listened casually. You have listened to it as a form of entertainment, as going to a cinema saying to yourselves, 'I disagree, I agree, it is a nice play, it was not nice', and so on. But if you also, which was your responsibility, worked as hard as the speaker, you would have said now, after an hour and a half; 'for God's sake, please, do let us stop!'

15th September 1968

TALKS AT CLAREMONT COLLEGES, CALIFORNIA, U.S.A.

1

IT WOULD BE rather interesting to know why most of you are here. Probably out of curiosity, or you have a genuine desire to find out what a man who comes from the East has to say. I think, first of all, it must be made quite clear that the speaker in no way represents India, Indian thought, Indian philosophy or any of that mysterious Oriental business.

I think it is important to establish a certain kind of communication between us; nowadays they talk a great deal about communication and make a lot of fuss about it. Surely it is fairly simple to communicate with one another; the difficulty lies in that each one of us unfortunately translates, compares or judges what is being said — in fact, we don't listen! On the other hand, if we listen attentively and seriously then communication becomes quite simple. One has only to say something, no matter how curious, and if you are at all serious, wanting to find out, you listen with care and attention, with a certain quality of affection, not only intellectually critical — which, of course, you must be — but also minutely examining and exploring everything that is being said. And to explore and listen attentively you must be *free* — free from the image, the tradition, the reputation which the speaker unfortunately has, so that you are capable of listening directly and immediately in order to understand. If, however, you try to follow a certain pattern of thought, certain tendencies in which you are caught, certain conclusions and prejudices which you have, then obviously all communication ceases.

It seems to me that right from the beginning it is very important to find out not only what the speaker has to say, but also how you listen. If you listen with a tendency to draw certain conclusions from what is being said, comparing it with what you already know, then what the speaker has to say merely becomes a matter of agreement or disagreement, a subject for mental examination or intellectual amusement. So during these talks if we could establish a right kind of relationship, a right kind of communication between yourselves and the speaker, then perhaps there might be a chance of going very deeply and seriously into this whole complex problem of living, to find out whether or not it is at all possible for human beings, who are so heavily conditioned, to change, to bring about within themselves an inward psychological revolution. And this is our main concern, not some Oriental philosophy or some kind of imaginative, conceptual thought-pattern leading to various conclusions and substituting old ideas for new ones.

I hope you will not mind my suggesting that it is very important to learn the art of listening. We don't listen, or if we do, we listen through a screen of words, of conceptual thoughts and conclusions, coloured by our own experience. And this screen obviously prevents us from listening which, as we said before, is a great art and one which apparently we have totally neglected. To listen so intimately, so completely, so intensely, that not only do we communicate, but go beyond and commune with one another like two friends who are very serious, very earnest about something. Communion is entirely different from communication; to commune we must not only understand the meaning of words, knowing full well that the word is never the thing nor is the description ever the described, but we must also be in that state of mind whose quality is attention and care, and a sense of intimate concern; and that can only take place when both of us are very serious.

Life demands great seriousness, not casual, occasional attention, but constant alertness and watchfulness because our problems are immense, so extraordinarily complex. It is only a very serious mind, a mind that is really earnest, capable of enquiry, and therefore free, that can find a solution to all our problems; and that is what we are going to do. We are not only going to communicate with each other verbally, but at a different level, we shall commune with one another, which seems much more important than mere verbal communication. So during these talks if we could look with clear eyes at this enormously complex business of living, look with eyes, that are young and fresh and innocent, then maybe our problems will have a totally different meaning. As I said previously, we must not only listen to the words, but also realise that the word is never the thing nor is the description ever the described. And to listen in this way there must be a quality of freedom, freedom from conclusions, from prejudices, from images and symbols, to enable both of us *to look* directly, intimately, intensely at the problems of our daily life, of our whole existence, in order to find out if it has any meaning at all.

One observes right throughout the world that all human beings, whatever their colour, creed or nationality, have their problems; problems of relationship, problems of living in a society that is so corrupt, which man has built over the centuries. Man himself is responsible for this structure, this society which is the product of his own hopes and demands, the result of his own violence, the outcome of his fears and ambitions, and in this structure we human beings are caught. And the structure is not different from the human being.

The society, whether in Europe, Asia or here in America, is not different or separate from each one of us; we *are* the society, we *are* the community, not only the individual, the human entity, but also the total, the collective. So there is no division, no separation between the society and ourselves; we are the world and the world is us and to bring about a radical revolution in society — which is absolutely essential — there must first of all be a radical transformation in our-

90

selves, and therefore we must enquire whether such a revolution in ourselves is at all possible. I am not using that word 'revolution' in its Communist, socialist or bloody sense, but I am speaking of a revolution which brings about a complete and radical transformation in the psyche itself, in the whole structure of the heart and mind. That is the central issue, not what the philosophers think or what the psychologists and analysts say; neither is it what the theologians assert nor what the believers or non-believers imagine.

The real issue then is whether human beings, as we are now, living in this complex and corrupt society with its wars, its struggles, its ambitions and competition, can bring about within ourselves a radical transformation, not gradually, that is through time, through many days or many years, but whether it is possible to change *immediately,* without accepting time at all. Apparently man has committed himself to war, to violence and this violence exists throughout the world, although in Asia and especially in India — where ideologies flourish as a fungus on damp ground — they talk a great deal about non-violence. And we human beings are committed to violence, to a way of life that leads to war, a way of life that is divided by religions and nationalities into beliefs, dogmas, rituals and extraordinary prejudices. Man is committed to this strange pattern of existence, righteously condemning one war, yet willing to take part in another; he is himself violent, brutal and aggressive which the anthropologists say he has inherited from the animal. Whatever the anthropologists or specialists say however has very little meaning, because we can examine and find out for ourselves the nature of our own violence, how brutal we are towards one another, not only verbally but in our thought and gesture. For thousands of years we have accepted a way of life that must inevitably lead to war, to wholesale slaughter, and we have not been able to change it; the politicians have tried but have never succeeded.

We are ordinary human beings — not specialists or experts

— living in this society and conditioned by our own background; we accept a way of life that is so corrupt, in which there is no love, not a single word of compassion. Observing all this, the problem then is whether it is at all possible for human beings, such as we are, to bring about a radical transformation within ourselves, and go further, to come upon that state which man has everlastingly sought and has called God or whatever name you wish to give it (names are not important).

Now, can human beings ever find this thing, or is it reserved only for the very few? We must first ask ourselves what place the religious mind has in the world to-day and whether it is possible to come upon this quality of love. You know, that word is so heavily laden with ugliness; it is like the word 'God', everybody uses it, the theologian, the grocer and the politician; the husband uses it for his wife, the boy for his girl friend and so on, but if you look at that word, go into it, you will see that it is the cause of so much suffering, so much misery, so much conflict and so many tortures; it also begets envy, jealousy and fear. One asks therefore whether the mind can be free of all this, so that there is a quality of love which is not corrupt, which is not made ugly by thought.

These are some of our problems: the relationship between man and man, whether a man can ever live at peace with himself and with his neighbour, whether there is a reality that is not put together by thought, whether there is such a quality of love, compassion and affection that has never been touched by jealousy, never tainted by fear, anxiety and guilt. Can the mind which is so heavily conditioned ever completely and totally free itself and discover, in that freedom, whether or not there is an ultimate reality? If we don't explore and find out for ourselves the truth of all this, then we must inevitably make life into a mechanical affair, a life in which there is constant struggle and which becomes utterly meaningless.

I am sure we are aware of all this; at least those of us who are serious must have asked ourselves this question, whether it is possible to uncondition the mind, so that it looks at life in a totally different way, so that it is no longer a Christian mind or a Buddhist mind, a Muslim or a Hindu mind, and all these other absurd divisions. Is it possible for such a conditioned mind ever to be free, to be innocent, and therefore vulnerable?

The main difficulty is that man lives in fragments, not only within himself, but outwardly; he is a scientist, a doctor, a soldier, a priest, a theologian, an expert or specialist of one kind or another. Inwardly his life is broken up, fragmentary; his mind, his intellect is at times cunning and clever, brutal and aggressive, while at other times it can be kind, gentle and affectionate. He tries to be moral — although the morality of society is utterly immoral — and his many desires tearing one against the other cause this fragmentation within and without, produce this contradiction inwardly as well as outwardly. And man is forever trying to bridge the gap, bring about an integration, which of course is absurd; there cannot be integration. If you examine that word and go behind it, you are forced to ask yourself who is the entity who is going to bring about this integration. Surely this entity who is going to integrate these many fragments is himself part of those fragments and therefore cannot possibly effect an integration between these various fragments. If one sees this clearly — namely that the broken parts of desire in this fragmentary, divided life can never be put together, can never be integrated, because the entity, the observer, who is trying to put them together is himself part of the fragmentation — then obviously there must be a different approach, which is *to see* the contradiction, the fragments, the opposing demands and conflicting desires, observe them and find out whether it is possible to go beyond them, and it is this *going beyond* which is the radical revolution. Then the mind is no longer torn, no

93

longer tortured; it is no longer in conflict with itself, and therefore with its neighbour, whether that neighbour be next door, in Russia or in Vietnam.

If one could observe this fact, because we are only dealing with facts, not with suppositions or ideals. Ideals have no meaning whatsoever; they are idiotic, the invention of a cunning clever mind when it cannot solve a problem like violence; so it invents non-violence as an ideal. Being unable to solve this problem of violence, and having created the ideal of non-violence that is, to be gentle, some time in the future, then that very invention of an ideal produces another conflict, another struggle, another state of contradiction.

So, it is important to observe the fact that we human beings are extraordinarily violent, that our culture, the society in which we live, our whole way of life with its greed, envy and competition, inevitably breed this violence. And it is even more important to be aware of this violence within oneself, actually to be aware of what is, not what should be, because the 'what should be' is a fiction, a myth, a romantic notion which all religions and idealists throughout the ages have nurtured and exploited. What good is the ideal of non-violence if I am full of violence? Please, this is very important to understand! Do listen quietly and attentively, don't automatically reject what is being said! You may be great idealists working for some cause, or you may have committed yourself to a certain formula, and you are suddenly confronted with a speaker who points out — politely but firmly — that all this is absurd. So it behoves one to listen, in order to find out; and to listen, one must put aside one's own particular formula, theory or myth. One can see quite clearly how ideals have divided man — the Christian ideal, the Hindu ideal and the Communist ideal — and according to their beliefs, they in their turn are split into innumerable sects, the Catholics and Protestants, and so on. Man therefore is held by ideals, he is a slave to them and consequently is incapable of observing

94

what is; he is always thinking about what should be.

The first demand then, the first challenge is to observe what is, which is to know yourself as you really are, not as you should be, that is a childish game, an immature struggle that has no meaning — but to look at violence and observe it. Can one look and how does one look? This is an extraordinarily difficult problem because there are certain factors which we must understand very clearly. Firstly, we must observe without identification, without the word, without the space between the observer and the thing observed; we must look without any image, without the thought, so that we are seeing things as they actually are. This is very important, because if we do not know how to look, how to observe what we are, then we will inevitably create conflict between what we see and the entity who sees. I hope this is fairly clear. I observe that I am violent in my speech, in my gestures and thoughts, and in my daily activities, both at home and in the office. Now I can only observe that I am violent if I do not attempt to escape from it or avoid it, and I will inevitably escape from it if I seek refuge in some ideal which says I must not be violent; because such an ideal is meaningless. When I say to myself I must not be violent, then there is the fact of my own violence and the ideal of what should be (that I must not be violent), hence there is a conflict between what is and what should be, and, for most of us, that is our life.

St. Paul

So it is important if we are at all serious — and life is only for those who are serious — to observe the nature and the structure of violence within ourselves, and to find out why we are violent. The mere discovery of the cause of violence does not end it, neither does analysis, however clever, however subtle, bring violence to an end, nor is it to be overcome by thinking about non-violence. Violence is merely a word, and the description of that violence is obviously not the fact. Please follow this! You may not be used to this kind of observation or exploration, you may prefer to leave it to the experts and just follow blindly, thereby creating an authority which becomes a terrible thing. If however you would be free of violence, which is buried so deep, you must first learn about yourself. You can only learn if you observe yourself — not according to Jung or Freud or some other specialist — then you are merely learning what they have already told you, so that is not learning at all. If you really want to learn about yourself, then you must put away all the comforting authority of others, and observe.

That observation is very complex, full of difficulties. First of all, is the observer different from the thing observed? I observe that I am violent, not only superficially, consciously but deep down; throughout my whole being I am violent. So I observe it in my speech, my walk, my gestures and in my ambitious drive to succeed. In this country particularly, success is praised to the heavens; we must succeed at all costs, but in the success there is a great deal of violence, aggression and brutality. So I see that I am violent and is this entity who observes different, separate from the violence, the thing he observes? Please *do* this as the speaker is explaining! If I may suggest, don't just listen to the words because words have no importance; what is important is to see whether or not the mind can ever be free from this terrible disease called violence, and in seeing it, is the seer, the observer different from the thing seen, the thing observed, or are the observer and the observed one? Do you understand all this? Is the observer who says 'I am violent' different from the violence itself? Obviously he is not, therefore what takes place? Do please follow this carefully if you are interested! What takes place when the observer realises that he himself *is* the violence which he has observed Then what is he to do to be free of that violence? I hope you understand the complexity of this problem and that we are communicating with each other.

Please, I am not trying to analyse you; that is something quite different and it has nothing whatever to do with what we are discussing. Now let's go into it step by step! When the observer finds out for himself that he *is* the observed, he *is* the violence, and that it is not something separate from him which he can change or control, then the division between the observer and the observed no longer exists, so the observer has instantly removed the cause of conflict and contradiction within himself. However the fact of violence remains — I am still violent by nature, my whole being is violent, and it is sheer nonsense to say that part of me is gentle and loving, while the other part is violent. Violence means division, contradiction, conflict, separateness, and a lack of love; but I have now realised the central fact, which is, that the observer is the observed, and is, therefore, no longer in conflict with the observed. I am the world and the world is me; I am the community and the community is me. So to bring about a radical transformation in society and in oneself, the observer must undergo a tremendous change — that is, to realise that the observer and the observed are one. Now can my mind observe the image of what I consider to be violence and also my vested interests in that violence, because the whole image I have about myself and the violence must disappear, so that the mind is free to observe. And after observing, the fact still remains that I am violent, even though I may say that I and the violence are one; so what am I to do? When I observe that I am violent and I see very clearly that the observer is that violence, then I realise I cannot possibly do anything at all, because any action whether it be positive or negative is still part of that violence.

Look, sirs, let's put it differently! There is this whole problem of egocentricity; we are enormously selfish, extraordinarily self-centred. We may go out of our way to help others, but deep down, the root, the core is this self-centred activity. It is like a tree whose main root has a thousand roots, and whatever the mind does or does not, nourishes this root. Am I making it clear, because we are dealing with a very complex problem, so please bear in mind what we said earlier — that the description is never the described. Mindful of this therefore one sees the necessity of being in *direct contact* with the fact of this egocentric operation that is going on all the time within each one of us, which is the action of separation, isolation, division and fragmentation, and whatever one does is part of that action, so one asks oneself whether there is a different kind of action, but the very asking of that question is still part of this fragmentation. One then realises one must look at violence in complete silence. *(Pause)* Is the speaker conveying anything at all? *(Assent)* Please don't agree, sir! This is not a matter of agreement or disagreement but a matter of perception on your part. The speaker is not important at all; what is important is for you to find out these things for yourself, so that you are free and not second-hand human beings. You must *look* to find out, to find out whether or not it is possible for the mind to be completely and totally free of this violence, pride and arrogance, and so come upon a different quality altogether. And to find that out you must look most intimately and discover for yourself; then it is your own, not somebody else's, not something that you have been told, because there is no teacher and no follower. Unfortunately that word 'guru' has been bandied about recently in this country; the word in Sanscrit means 'the one who points', like a signpost by the roadside. However you don't worship that post, hang garlands around it; neither do you follow it around and carry out all the mysterious orders a guru is supposed to give; he is just a signpost by the roadside, you read and pass by.

So, you have to be your own teacher and your own disciple, and there is no teacher outside, no saviour, no master; you yourself have to change and, therefore, you have to learn to observe, to know yourself. This learning about yourself is a fascinating and joyous business; it is to learn about violence which is part of the structure of your life. And to learn, the mind must be free; it cannot learn about violence if you have already accumulated knowledge about violence. That is one of the things we have done with our learning; knowledge and learning are two different things. The doctor, the scientist, the engineer have accumulated knowledge and they add to it as new discoveries are made, and therefore their knowledge becomes a storehouse, a tradition, but that is not learning; learning is only possible in a state of constant movement, it only takes place in the *active present*. Learning is a movement, whether you are learning in a college or learning about yourself; you are learning as you go along, not *having learnt* and then applying what you have learnt, what you have accumulated; that is not learning at all, that is merely the accumulation of knowledge.

And in that learning there is great joy, there is no despair at what you see, because you are not comparing it with your ideal, with what you should be; there is only *what is*, and to observe what is, your learning is infinite. Everything is in you — like the speaker, you don't have to read any book — because man is as old as the hills, and more. He is a living thing and a living thing is not to be conditioned, but we *have* conditioned it, and that is why our life has become such a torture, such a meaningless struggle.

I wonder if you would like to ask any questions. You know, to ask a question one must be completely sceptical about everything, including what the speaker says; the speaker has no authority whatsoever, and one must be sceptical, although, of course, one must know when to let go of the leash so that one is not sceptical all the time. Obviously you must ask questions but you must ask the right question, which is a most difficult thing to do. Please, this does not mean that I am trying to stop you asking questions! It is very important to ask a really extraordinary question, one which taxes you to the full, a question which is true *to you*, not to the speaker or to anybody else; obviously you must

99

ask that kind of question, but at the same time you must never wait for an answer from another because no one can *answer* your question; it is only fools who give advice. So please ask a serious question, not something irrelevant without any depth or meaning!

Questioner: You have talked about silence, and occasionally my mind is silent, but what is this silence you speak about?

KRISHNAMURTI: The speaker *can* tell you what that silence is, but unless it is yours, it will have very little meaning. Silence is absolutely necessary to look, to listen, and to observe; if your mind is chattering — and our minds are everlastingly chattering — how can you possibly listen? How can you possibly look at a tree, at a cloud or a bird without that silence? If you want to look at a tree, or the light on a cloud, naturally your mind must be silent, but you can't force it, simply because you want to see the beauty of the tree. It is very important to look, to see without the image and you must be silent to look at your husband or your wife without the image; you are no longer silent, however, if you carry with you the image of your husband or your wife. It is only in silence that you learn and *love* is completely silent.

This love is unknown to us because thought, which breeds pleasure and fear, is always casting a shadow over everything. This silence is part of meditation (we are not going into that now because it involves a great deal), but without understanding meditation, the beauty of it, the ecstasy of it and its very benediction, life has no meaning. Meditation is not something separate from every day life, nor is it learning some trick in a monastery, whether it be Zen or some other religion, because meditation is a way of life, and part of this immense silence about which we were speaking. Perhaps during these three public talks we shall be able to discuss meditation, as well as what love is and what death is.

Questioner: Could we discuss observation without the observer?

KRISHNAMURTI: What is the observer? Please, find out! Let's go into it together! Don't just listen and accept or reject, but let both of us take the journey together. What *is* the observer? The observer is the experience whether it be the experience of yesterday or of a thousand yesterdays. The observer is the accumulated knowledge, memory; the observer is essentially the tradition, the past, the dead ashes of many thousand yesterdays. The observer is the one who says I am hurt, I am angry, I have been insulted, this is my view, that is my opinion, the one who thinks and is caught up in formulas; all that is the observer. So the observer is *essentially* the past, and can you look, observe without the past? Can you observe a tree? Let's begin with something simple! Can you observe a tree without the past? Can you observe a tree, a cloud, a bird outwardly, without the past, which means without the word, without your knowledge, without all the images you have about the tree, about the cloud, about the bird. So can you look *without the past?* It is comparatively easy to look at some familiar object without the past, without yesterday, but can you look at your wife or at your husband without the image of the past, the hurts and the nagging, the quarrels and the brutality, the pleasures and the delights and the various forms of hidden and unexpressed demands, hopes and fears. Can you look without all this, so that you are looking with fresh eyes. It is quite an arduous task because it demands attention, it demands the joy of learning.

We human beings have no relationship with one another, with our husbands or wives, no matter how intimate we may be, no matter how many times we have slept together. We have images, and the relationship is between two images, not between human beings because human beings are living things, and it is very dangerous, uncertain, to have a relationship with a living thing; above all we want to be certain in our relationship. That's why we say I *know* my wife or my husband, my neighbour or my friend. And to look without the observer, which means looking without the past, without the memory, without all the accumulated hopes and fears, the pleasure and enjoyment, the sorrow and despair — to look in such a manner is the beginning of love.

8th November 1968.

2

THE LAST TIME we met we were discussing this question of violence; how it has pervaded all our lives from childhood until we die. This violence, this aggression, this brutality exists right throughout the world not only in the individual, where it manifests as hatred and in twisted forms of loyalty, but also outwardly in our acceptance of war as a way of life. Violence arises from rights of property, sexual rights and other forms of ideological beliefs. One is quite familiar with all this; one sees it very clearly.

All the religions have said: don't kill, be kind, be compassionate, and so on, but organised religions have no meaning whatsoever; they never had. So we are confronted with this issue — the problem of violence. And one must ask whether it is at all possible for a human being, not only in his personal relationship, but in his relationship to society to be completely free of this violence. This is not a rhetorical question, nor an intellectual enquiry but an actual problem that faces each one of us both psychologically, inwardly (inside the skin, as it were) and also outwardly, in the home and at the office. In every form of activity there is this aggressive spirit with its engendering hatred and animosity. And we were asking whether it is at all possible, not only at the conscious level but also at the deeper levels of the mind, to eradicate this violence completely, so that we can live at peace with one another and go beyond the national divisions, the religious separation with its dogmas, beliefs, theories and ideologies.

Now let us approach this problem another way. One of our main difficulties, it seems to me, is that although we have plenty of energy, apparently we lack the drive, the vitality, and enthusiasm to bring about this change within ourselves. After all, knowing ourselves — not according to some specialist — is the most important thing; that is the basis of all action, and if we do not know ourselves, study ourselves, learn about ourselves, and go deeply into that meditative spirit within ourselves, then there is no foundation, then all action becomes fragmentary, contradictory and out of this state of contradiction there arises conflict, and it is this conflict which burdens each one of us. Everything we do, everything we think, everything we touch breeds conflict and struggle which in various forms does waste energy that is absolutely vital for this inward psychological revolution. This implies that we shall be completely free from conflict within ourselves; but it does not mean merely to be content, to vegetate or lead a cow-like existence; on the contrary, when energy is not used for mischievous purposes, as it is now, that energy is the transforming element in knowing ourselves. Although the ancient Greeks, the Hindus, and the Buddhists have all said: 'Know thyself', very few people have ever bothered to go into it and find out. To learn about oneself no authority is necessary, whether it be of the Church, of a Saviour or Master, or of some specialist; all that one has to do — if one is really serious and earnest — is to observe, not only critically but with a mind that is free to learn. *(A baby cries)* Who shall have the voice?

✳ You know, in India where we speak in the open, there are about three or four thousand people who bring their children with them; there are also students, beggars and every form of humanity; most of them do not understand English, but it is considered worthwhile, worthy of merit, to attend a religious meeting, so there is a great deal of noise, and the crows and the other birds join in. Everybody shares in this kind of reunion, not only the birds and children, but also those who have little knowledge of anything, and do not understand very much, but all the same it is good to attend such a gathering. Here where English is spoken and understood, it is worthwhile and significant that children as well as the aged, and those in middle life, should come together to talk over seriously and intimately the problems that confront each one of us.

Unfortunately we are not sufficiently serious, we are prejudiced and have reached certain conclusions which prevent us from examining ourselves. Our experience acts as a barrier, as does our knowledge, so if we could listen with a quality of mind that is both earnest and enquiring, then in this communication we shall not merely be listening to a lot of words or gathering a new set of ideas, but rather we shall be penetrating deeply within ourselves and learning about ourselves.

Surely the intention of these meetings is to go deeply into ourselves and *discover ourselves,* not to be told what to do and what to think (which is too immature, too childish), not to create another authority, another guru and all that absurd business. Self-discovery is not asking 'Who am I?' but actually observing yourself as you would look at your face in a mirror, observing your actions, your gestures and the words you use, observing the way you look at a tree, at a bird or a passing cloud, at your wife, your husband or a neighbour. So through observation one begins to discover what one is, because one is never static; there is nothing permanent within, although the theologians and the other 'godly' people assert that there is a constant entity, which again is a theory, an idea. If we could then enquire, joyfully and freely, whether the mind — this human mind which has lived for millions of years and has been so heavily conditioned by a thousand experiences, which has embraced and accepted so many ideas and ideologies — whether such a mind can go into itself and find out whether or not it can be completely and totally free from violence.

105

Now let us approach this problem differently! As long as there is fear, there must be violence, aggression, hatred and anger. Most human beings are afraid, not only outwardly but also inwardly, although the outer and the inner are not separate, they are really one movement; so if we understand the inner — its design, its nature and the whole structure of fear — then perhaps we shall be able to bring about a different society, a different culture, because the present society is corrupt and its morality is immoral.

So we have to find out, not ideologically, not intellectually as a kind of game, but actually discover for ourselves whether or not it is possible to be free from this fear. There are various forms of fear, too numerous to go into — the fear of darkness, the fear of losing one's job or one's livelihood, the fear of being found out when you have done something of which you are ashamed, the wife's fear of the husband, the husband's fear of the wife, the parent's fear of the children, the fear of not being loved, the fears of old age, of loneliness and death; so many forms of fear. So unless we understand fear, the central issue of fear, we shall live in darkness and, therefore, we shall never be free from this brutality, aggression, envy and competition.

What is fear? What is the actual state of fear itself, not the various forms of fear? What causes fear? Please, as we said previously, the speaker is not an analyst, he is not carrying out an analysis en masse. We are not concerned with analysis at all, because as you will see presently analysis is a waste of time. Analysis postulates an analyser and a thing to be analysed whereas the analyser himself *is* the analysed; he cannot possibly separate himself from the thing he wishes to analyse, so when he observes this phenomenon he sees what a dreadful waste of time analysis is. You may — if you are rich and it takes your fancy — indulge in it as a kind of game to amuse yourself, but if you really want to go beyond the nature and structure of fear, eradicate it altogether, you must come to it, not through any analytical process or intellectual design, but *directly*. If you would understand something, especially a living thing, you must observe it with a living mind, not with dead knowledge, not with something that you have already learnt or that you already know.

So that's what we are going to do and in listening, you are not listening to the speaker at all, because he is of no importance whatsoever. He is like the telephone — it is not important! What is important is *what the telephone is saying*. It is necessary then to observe yourself, to observe your own mind *through* the words of the speaker, using him as a mirror. And when you observe yourself as a human being, so heavily conditioned by the past, so inextricably caught in sorrow and travail, then out of that observation there comes an understanding which produces a totally different kind of action, and we are going to explore that action together, discuss it, talk it over, not as teacher and pupil or guru and disciple, but rather as two friends trying to solve the immense problems of everyday life. If you don't lay a sane, healthy, decent and righteous foundation, you cannot go very far, you cannot possibly meditate or find out what is truth.

To lay the right foundation, so that we become a light to ourselves, we must understand fear. What is fear (not how to overcome fear)? I do not know if you have noticed that anything that has to be overcome must be overcome again and again. If you have ever conquered anything — it doesn't matter what it is, some outward or inward enemy — you have to re-conquer it over and over again. We are not trying to *overcome* fear, nor are we trying to suppress it or give it a different quality, but instead we are trying to understand it, trying to find out what fear actually is and how it comes into being. So what is this fear, the fear of what has been, the fear of yesterday, the fear of tomorrow, the fear of not being and not becoming; that is, fear in time. If you are faced with a challenge, an enormous crisis in your life — and there is no yesterday and no tomorrow — you act *instantly,* don't you? It is the thinking about what happened yesterday or what will happen tomorrow that breeds fear, but when your action is immediate, you cannot think about what is happening *now,* at this instant; thought cannot enter into the active present. It is only when the action is over and done with, that you can think of what might have been, of the past or of the future. So thought is the cause of fear, thinking about the past and the future, thinking about yesterday and tomorrow — I had pain yesterday and tomorrow perhaps it will return or tomorrow I may lose my job, so I am afraid. Please, observe your own mind and heart! Go into it yourself and you will see how extraordinarily simple it becomes! If you don't do it, then it is very complex, then it has no meaning whatsoever.

Therefore thought breeds the fear — the thought that perhaps I am no good and I may not succeed — the thought of being unloved and my utter loneliness — the thought of being found out in some shameful act I have committed — the thought of losing something which is very precious and dear to me. So in its wake thought brings regret and despair. As well as being the source of fear, thought is also the source of pleasure. The thought of something which has given you enjoyment nourishes that pleasure, gives substance to it. When you see the sunset of an evening or the early morning light on the hills and you take in all its beauty and loveliness, or in the surrounding stillness you hear the sound of a quail, when this happens, at the actual moment of perception, there is no thought, only a total awareness of everything around you. But when you start to think about it, go back to it in thought, and say to yourself, I must have more of this pleasure, re-capture the beauty of it, then the thinking about it gives further enjoyment. So thought breeds pleasure as well as fear; this is an obvious psychological fact which intellectually we accept, but that acceptance has no value, because pleasure contains within it the seed of fear; so pleasure *is* fear.

Please watch this very carefully! We are not saying you must deny yourself pleasure. All the religions throughout the world have condemned pleasure, sexual or otherwise — we are not saying that! A religious man does not deny or suppress but rather he is learning, observing.

So thinking about what has happened or what might happen brings fear, as with the fear of death for instance — postponed or put away into the distant future — but it is *there*. And thinking about some shortcoming in one's past which others might use to their advantage, or thinking about the pleasure of sex and keeping the image alive. This thinking about something does breed either fear or pleasure.

The question then arises: is it possible to live our everyday life without the interference of thought? It is not such a crazy question as it sounds and it is a very important question, because man throughout the ages has worshipped thought and the intellect in all the 'clever' books with their theories, in all the theological works with their concepts about God, showing us the right way to live. These experts and specialists are like people who are tethered to a post; they are restricted from going any further because of their conditioning, so whatever they think, they are limited. And because they are the result of ten thousand years of propaganda, their gods, their dogmas and rituals have no meaning whatsoever. Man has worshipped thought, put it on a pedestal. Look at all the books that have been written!

Now what is thought and what significance has it? I know there are people who have said 'Kill the mind!' You can't kill it! You can't just drop thought as though it were some garment you are wearing. You have to understand this extraordinary process of thinking, *your own thinking,* not by studying books or being lectured to about thought. When you think at all, what is the origin of thinking? When is thought necessary and when is it not? When is it an impediment and when is it a help? So, you must find out all these things for yourself, not be guided by the speaker or some other authority.

You know, the world is becoming more and more authoritarian, not only religiously and politically but psychologically. There must, of course, be a certain kind of authority in technological knowledge, but to wield authority in religious and psychological matters is an abomination; then man is never free and never *can* be free, and freedom is an absolute necessity. How can a mind that is afraid ever be free? How can a mind that is clouded by perpetual thinking and incessant chattering ever be free to look, to enquire, to live and to know that ecstasy which is not of pleasure. So what is thought and can thought come to an end at a certain level and yet function at other levels rationally, sanely, objectively, nonemotionally and impersonally? That is, knowledge about the universe, about everything is necessary — *knowledge,* but one also observes that thought breeds fear as well as pleasure, so one asks oneself, can this thought come to an end. Once again you have to find this out for yourselves, so that you are no longer second-hand human beings — as you are now — but you are discovering it for yourselves. So what is thought? Surely this is very simple; thought is the response of memory. Someone asks you a familiar question and you reply immediately; and if the question is a little more complex then you take time before answering. During the interval between the question and the answer memory is in operation and from that memory you reply; so thinking is the response of memory and memory is the storehouse of thousands of experiences, both conscious as well as unconscious. That is, the unconscious is the vast storehouse as memory of the race, of the tradition, whether it be Christian, Hindu or Buddhist, and therein is hidden the accumulation of many centuries, while the conscious mind is the storehouse of knowledge you have acquired. And through this whole structure of memory you are conditioned and from that conditioning you respond; if

110

you are conditioned as a Republican, a Democrat or a Communist then from that background, from that memory you respond. If you are brought up as a Christian and have been indoctrinated by the propaganda of the church with its dogmas and rituals, then you respond according to that memory, that conditioning; or if you are a Hindu, then you respond from the background of your gods and your puja, the rites of the temple and so on.

Please follow this! It may appear to be complicated but it is only *verbally* complex. So thought is the response of the brain cells which have accumulated knowledge as experience and since thought breeds fear, it has divided itself and separated the thinker from the thought. The thinker says 'I am afraid'. The thinker, the 'I' is separate from the thing of which he is afraid, the fear itself, so there is duality, a division — the thinker and the thought, the observer and the observed, the experiencer and the experienced. This duality or division, this separation is the cause of effort, the source from which all effort springs. Apart from obvious duality as man and woman, black and white, there is an inward psychological duality as the observer and the observed, the one who experiences and the thing experienced. In this division, in which time and space are involved, is the whole process of conflict; you can observe it in yourself. You are violent, that is a fact and you also have the ideological concept of non-violence, so there is duality. Now the observer says 'I must become non-violent' and the attempt to become non-violent *is* conflict, which is a waste of energy; whereas if the observer is totally aware of that violence — without the ideological concept of non-violence — then he is able to deal with it immediately.

One must observe therefore this dualistic process at work within oneself — this division of the I and the not-I, the observer and the observed, and thought has brought about this division. It is thought which says, I am dissatisfied with what is and I shall only be satisfied with what should be; it is

111

thought which has enjoyed some experience as pleasure and says I must have more of it. So in each one of us there is this dualistic, contradictory process and this process is a waste of energy. Therefore one asks oneself — and I hope you are asking — why is there this division? Why is there this constant effort between what is and what should be? And is it possible to eradicate totally the what should be, the ideal, which is the future, as well as the what has been, the past, from which the future is built? Is there an observer at all except as thought dividing itself into the observer and the observed? You can either look at this and discard it or look at it and go into it very deeply, because as long as there is an observer, there must be division, hence conflict. And the observer is always the past, never new; the thing observed may be new, but the observer always translates it in terms of the old, the past, so thought can never be new and therefore never free. Thought is always the old, so when you worship thought, you are worshipping something which is dead; thought is like the children of barren women. And we who are supposed to be great thinkers actually live on the past and therefore we are dead human beings.

Thought then has created pleasure and also fear, which breeds violence, so the problem is: there is fear and there is violence, and by considering them merely in terms of words, or by description, does not bring them to an end. I see very clearly how thought has bred this fear — I am afraid I may lose something which is very precious to me, that is the thought which has produced this fear. If thought suppresses itself, says 'I won't think about it' the fear is still there. Please follow this slowly! If I attempt to escape from it, accept or deny it, I am still afraid, it is still there. So what is the next question? There is fear and thought cannot be suppressed; that would be an extreme form of neurosis.

What takes place when the observer is the observed? Do you understand the question? The observer is the result of

112

the past, of thought; and the thing observed, which is fear, is also the result of thought, so the observer and the observed are both the product of thought. Now whatever thought does with regard to this state of fear — whether it accepts or suppresses it, whether it interferes and tries to sublimate it, *whatever it does* — is to continue fear in a different form. So thought, observing this whole process, learning intimately about itself (not being told by another), seeing for itself the nature and structure of fear, *which is itself,* thought then realises that whatever it does with regard to fear is still to give nourishment to fear. So then what happens, what comes out of this understanding?

I hope you are following all this. I have observed fear — which is thought — as I have observed pleasure. Now the observer *is* the observed, although thought has separated the observer and the thing observed. I see that very clearly; there is an understanding of it, not as an intellectual concept but as an actual reality, so what takes place? The understanding is not intellectual therefore it is the highest form of intelligence and to be intelligent, in this way, means to be highly sensitive, aware of the nature and the whole structure of fear. If I suppress fear or run away from it, then there is no sensitive perception of fear and all its implications, therefore I must learn about fear and not run away; and I can only learn about something when I am in *direct contact* with it, and I can only be in contact with it so intimately when I can look freely. This freedom is the highest form of sensitivity, not only physically but in the mind also; the brain itself becomes highly sensitive. This understanding is intelligence and it is this intelligence which is going to operate and as long as there is this intelligence, there is no fear; fear only comes when this intelligence is absent. This must be understood at a very deep level not just verbally, because as we said previously the word is not the thing and the description is never the described. You can describe food to a hungry man but the words and the description do not appease his hunger. This intelligence is the highest form of sensitivity, not only at the physical level (this implies a great deal which unfortunately we haven't time to go into), but also at the deeper psychological level, and it is this intelligence which is the foundation of virtue.

Nowadays, I am afraid, most people spit on that word 'virtue' as they do on 'humility' and 'kindliness' — they have lost all their meaning. But without virtue there is no order; we are not talking of political order or economic order, but of something quite different; the order of which we are speaking *is* virtue, not the so-called virtue or morality of the church and society, because they are based on authority. The morality of the church and organised religions is immoral because it compromises with society; to these organisations virtue is an ideal, but you cannot cultivate humility. So order is virtue and this order can only come into being when we understand the whole negative process of disorder which is in ourselves, which is this contradiction, this division which has been brought about by the process of thought. Unless we understand this state of order and virtue very clearly and lay its foundation deeply within ourselves, there is no possibility of of going into the question of meditation, and of finding out what love is and what truth is.

And now if you have time and the inclination, perhaps you would like to ask questions and talk things over together.

Questioner: Could you discuss this verbalization which takes place within oneself when one wishes to look at something very clearly?

KRISHNAMURTI: I wonder if we have ever observed within ourselves what slaves we are to words, to verbalization? Why? We are incapable of looking at anything — a cloud, a bird, those marvellous hills over there, our wife or our husband — without this process of verbalization. Why? Why is it that we cannot look at anything without the image? To understand this is quite a complex problem. Why do we look at everything through an image which is the word? Why do I look at my wife or my husband, or at my friend, with an image? My wife has done a great many things — she has possessed me, nagged me, bullied me or annoyed me, insulted me and discarded me. And through time, through many days I have put all this together; it has become a memory and through that memory, of all these hurts, I look at her. If I may point out, the speaker unfortunately has a certain reputation and through that image you look at him and therefore you are not looking at the speaker at all; you are looking through the image you have about the speaker, the image being the word, the idea, the tradition. So can you look at something without the image? Can you look at someone without the image? Can you look, without the image, at your wife or your husband, at the man across the valley, at the man who has insulted you or flattered you?

It is only possible to look without the image when you have understood the nature of experience. What is experience? *(Pause)* I hope you are all doing this with me and not just listening to a lot of words! You must understand what experience is, because it is this accumulated experience which is all the time building images — so what is experience? The word 'experience' means to go right through something, but we never do! Let us take it at the simplest level! You insult me and the experience remains, leaves an imprint on my mind, becomes part of my memory, so you are my enemy; I don't like you. And the same thing happens if you flatter me, then you are my friend; the memory of the flattery remains as does the insult. Please follow this very carefully! Can I, at the moment of the flattery or the insult, go through it completely, so that the experience leaves no mark on the mind at all? This means that when you insult me, I listen to it and look at it, totally, completely, objectively and without emotion, as I look at this microphone, which means giving total attention

115

to it with my whole mind and heart, to find out if what you say is true and if it isn't, then what is the point of holding on to it. This is not a theory; the mind is never free if there is any form of conceptual thinking or image-building. And I do the same if you flatter me, say what a marvellous speaker I am. I listen with my whole mind and heart *while you are speaking,* not afterwards, to find out why you are saying it and what value it has, whether or not I am a marvellous speaker, then I have both finished with insult and flattery. However it is not as simple as that, because we enjoy living in a world of images, images of like and dislike; we live with those images and our minds are forever chattering, forever verbalizing, so we never look at our wife, our husband or the mountain with a free mind, and it is only the innocent mind that can look.

Questioner: How can we get rid of this division in ourselves?

KRISHNAMURTI: First of all, if I may suggest, don't *get rid* of anything! Getting rid of something is to escape from it. You have to look at it, go into it! Now this division of like and dislike, love and hate, mine and not mine exists within oneself — why?

We come now to a very important point, which is, do you understand or discover anything through analysis? Let us look at it! There is this problem of division, contradiction within ourselves and I want to understand it, go into it to find out if it is possible for the mind to be completely non-fragmentary. Now can I find out through analysis? Will this division come to an end through analysis? Surely analysis implies an analyser and the thing to be analysed, therefore the analyser is different from the analysed and in that there is division; so can this fragmentation within ourselves come to an end through analysis, which is of course thought, or does it come about through having direct perception?

You can only have direct perception when there is no

condemnation of this division, when there is no evaluation, saying I must be in this state in which there is no division at all, I must achieve this harmony; you can't achieve harmony as long as this division between you and harmony exists as an idea, because that division, which is brought about by thought, breeds further division.

Since ancient times they have said there is God and there is man — this everlasting division. Later on they said God is not over there, he's here, in you; and again there was this division between you and the God within you. The God who previously was in a stone, in a tree, in a statue, who was venerated as the Saviour, as the Master was now in you; you *are* the God. Then the God within you says do this, don't do that, be harmonious, be kind, love your neighbour, but you can't because there is a division between you and the God within you.

So thought is the entity that divides and through thought, that is through analysis, you hope to come upon that state in which there is no division at all; you can't do it, it can only come about when the mind itself sees and understands this whole process, and is then completely quiet. That word 'understanding' is very important; a description doesn't bring understanding, neither does finding out the cause of something. So what brings understanding? What *is* understanding? Have you ever noticed when your mind is quietly listening — not arguing, judging, criticizing, evaluating, comparing but just listening, then in that state the mind is silent and then only understanding comes. There is this division within ourselves, this everlasting contradiction and we must simply be aware of it, and not try to do anything about it, because whatever we do causes this division. So complete negation is complete action.

10th November 1968

3

∧ THIS IS THE last talk so, if I may, I would like to go into something which might be slightly foreign to you although perhaps you have heard the word and given it a special significance. I am speaking of meditation and it is one of the most important things to understand, so if we can, then perhaps we shall also be able to understand the whole complex problem of existence, and live it. In existence is included all relationship, not only the relationship between ourselves and our property, but our relationship with each other and also our relationship, if there is any, to reality.

In this troublesome and complex existence, understanding is absolutely essential. I am not using the word 'understanding' in its literal sense because to me understanding means the very *doing* itself; you do not understand first and then do, but the understanding *is* the doing, *is* the action; the two are not separate. In the understanding of this whole problem perhaps we shall also come upon that word 'love' and, maybe, the thing which most human beings dread, death.

So we are going to explore, look together into this question of life, of existence, in which is included all relationship, love and death. Meditation is the approach to the understanding of this problem of living, not merely as a phenomenon, but as something tremendously significant, greatly to be cherished and deeply lived, in fact meditation *is* the living. Many people however treat meditation as an escape from life, that is they retire into a monastery, put on a special garb and withdraw completely from this whole complex business of living. There are certain schools in India and in Asia where they offer a

118

method, a system, a way which perhaps will give a greater sensitivity and, if you are foolish enough to have visions, will enable you to escape into some mysterious metaphysical existence which in reality is still the same old sordid life. But meditation has no way, no system, no method; it is not an abstraction of life with all its delights, its sorrows and despair, nor is it an avoidance, an escape into some mystical, non-realistic, romantic world of one's own imagination.

So we are not, at least the speaker is not using that word as a means of escape, but rather as an approach to the understanding of the whole of existence, then meditation has great significance, then it becomes a benediction, an extraordinary thing which must be understood at the deepest level. So let us go into it together! You know, recently that word has become very fashionable; it is almost on every lip, one even sees it in The New Yorker and the long-haired gentlemen talk about it a great deal. They offer you a method, a system, give you a few words to repeat as a mantra, and assure you that through this practice you will transcend all your sorrows and achieve some extraordinary reality, which is of course obviously nonsense, because a dull, stupid mind that is so heavily conditioned, sodden by its own superstitions, prejudices and conclusions, can follow a certain method and meditate indefinitely, but it will still remain a dull, stupid mind. Through examination we can see the utter futility of the method, the 'how', the pattern, whether it is laid down by the ancients, or by the modern guru with all his pretensions and the utter absurdity of offering a state which is generally called enlightenment in exchange for a sum of money. So we won't concern ourselves any further with this kind of meditation, which is a form of escape; we can objectively and intelligently put it aside.

Let us be clear from the very beginning that meditation is not a form of entertainment; it is not something you purchase from another whatever the price, neither is it the acceptance of authority of any kind, including that of the speaker, especially that of the speaker, because in understanding this extraordinary problem of living, there is *no* authority, no teacher, no master and no guru; they have all failed. Each one of us is in sorrow, is in travail; we are confused, miserable, striving after something and it is essential to understand this rather than some mysterious vision. Visions are very easily explained and through the use of drugs, through the repetition of words and phrases, through the practice of various forms of self-hypnosis, the mind *can* produce any fantasy, believe in anything, and play innumerable tricks upon itself.

We are concerned with life, and with the living of that life every day, with its painful struggles and fleeting pleasures, with its fears, hopes, despair and sorrow, with the aching loneliness and the complete absence of love, with the crude and subtle forms of selfishness, and with the ultimate fear of death. So it is that which directly concerns us and to understand it deeply, with all the passion at our disposal, meditation is the key, but not the meditation given by another, put together by some book, by some philosopher or specialist, because the quality of meditation is very important. The word itself means to ponder over, to think over, to enter deeply into an issue. Meditation then is not how to think or what to do to control the mind so that it becomes quiet and silent, but rather the understanding of all life's problems, so that the beauty of silence comes into being, because without this quality of beauty, life has no significance at all. I do not mean by beauty, the beauty of those mountains, of those trees, the beauty of the light over the water or the bird on the wing, but the beauty in living, to come upon it in your daily life whether you are in the office or at home, when you are walking by yourself communing with nature and the world, because without that beauty life is utterly meaningless.

So let us together go into this question, not only objectively, outwardly but also inwardly. The outward movement *is* the inward as well, the two are not separate; they are like the outgoing and incoming tide and to understand them, not separate or divided, is the beauty of meditation. Therefore what is required to live *totally,* in which there is no strife, no contradiction, is balance and harmony, and meditation is the way.

Many things are involved in meditation; I hope you are interested in all this because it is one of the most important things to understand. If you do not know how to meditate, how to live — I am afraid most of us lead a very superficial life, going to the office, having a good job, having a family and a home, being entertained either at a cocktail party or at the cinema, and this we call living — then your life becomes a very dull, empty, shallow affair. Unfortunately modern civilization, especially in this country, is becoming more and more standardised, more superficial. You may have all the luxuries in the world, good food, good houses, good bathrooms, and enjoy good health, but without the inward life, not the *second-hand* inward life of another, but an inward life of your own, which you have discovered for yourself, which you have cherished, which you are living and which *is* meditation, then life becomes a very shoddy business; then we shall have more wars, more destruction and more misery; so meditation, whether you like it or not, is absolutely essential for every human being, whatever he is, whether he is highly sophisticated or a simple person by the wayside, so I hope we can enter and take this journey together.

Meditation involves concentration, which if one observes it, is a way of exclusion; that is, concentration implies forcing thought in one particular direction and excluding everything else; that is generally what is meant by concentration. You focus and direct the mind upon something and that concentration builds a wall, erects a barrier which prevents any other thought from entering, and in doing that there is a dualistic process at work, a division, a contradiction, which is fairly

121

obvious if you look at it. So meditation is something other than concentration and control of thought although, of course, concentration is necessary. Meditation involves attention, which is not concentration, although concentration is included in attention. *To attend* — that means to give your whole mind, your heart and your body passionately to something and in that attention, if you observe very carefully, there is neither the thinker nor the thought, neither the observer nor the observed, but only a state of attention; and to attend so completely, so freely, there must be freedom.

Here then is the whole problem: it is only a mind which is totally free that can give complete attention, that can attend both intellectually and emotionally, aware of all its responses, from which comes freedom. And this is not so difficult, if you don't give it an extraordinary meaning; it is really very simple. When you listen to anything — whether to music or to the weird cry of the coyotes as they call to each other of an evening, whether to the song of a bird or to the voice of your husband or wife — then give complete attention to it, and *you do* when the challenge is very great, immediate, then you listen with extraordinary attention. When it is painful or profitable, when you are going to get something out of it, you listen very attentively; but when there is a reward in that listening, there is always the fear of losing.

Therefore in attention there is freedom, and only a free mind is capable of that quality of attention in which there is no achieving, no gaining or losing, and no fear. And a quiet, attentive mind is absolutely essential to understand this immense problem of living and come upon that state of love. So together we are going to learn what it means to attend, for it is only the attentive mind that is the meditative mind; we are going *to learn,* not accumulate knowledge; accumulating knowledge is one thing and learning quite another, so we are going to learn together about this problem of living, which is relationship, which is love and which is death.

What is living? Not what living *should be,* not what is the purpose, the goal of living, not what is the significance of living, not what is the principle upon which life should be based, but what actually is living, as it is now, at this moment, in the privacy and secrecy of our daily life, because that is the only fact, and nothing else; everything else is theoretical, unreal and illusory. So what is this life, our life, the life of a private human being? What is the life of a private human being in relationship to the society which he has built and which holds him prisoner? Surely he *is* the society, he *is* the world, and the world is not different from him, which is another obvious fact.

We are actually dealing with *what is,* with our own life and not with abstractions, not with ideals which are idiotic anyway. So what is our living? From the moment we are born until we die, our life is a constant battle, a never ending struggle, full of fear, loneliness and despair, a wearisome routine of boredom and repetition and a total lack of love, relieved occasionally by a fleeting pleasure. This is our life, our daily tortured existence, spending forty years in an office or factory, or being a housewife with its drudgery and dull care, with its envy and jealousy, the utter boredom of it all, fearing failure and worshipping success, and everlastingly thinking about the sexual pleasure. So that is the pattern of our life if you are at all serious and observe what actually is. If however you are merely seeking entertainment in different forms, either in church or on the football field, then such entertainment brings its own pain, its own sorrow, its own problems, and the superficial mind *does* escape through the church and through football, but we are not dealing with such a superficial mind because it is not really interested.

Life is serious, but in that seriousness there is great laughter and it is only the serious mind that is living, that can solve the immense problems of existence. Our life then, as it is lived daily, is a travail; no one can deny it and we don't know what to do about it; we want to find a way of living differently; at least we say we do, and some of us make an attempt to change it. Before making any attempt to change, we must understand actually what is, not what should be; we must actually take *what is* in our hands and look at it, and you cannot do that, come closely and intimately in contact with it, if you have an ideal, or if you say this must be changed into that, or if you are intent on changing. If however you are capable of looking at it *as it is,* then you will find quite a different quality of change, so that's what we are going to investigate.

First of all, we must actually see what our daily life is at this moment, to see it, not shyly or with reluctance, but without pain and resistance. It is *that* — a travail! Can we look at it, live with it? Can we make intimate contact, be in direct relationship with it? Here is our difficulty! To be in direct relationship with something, there must be *no* image between you and the thing you observe; the image being the word, the symbol, the memory of what it was yesterday or a thousand yesterdays ago. Let us put it very simply. The relationship that you have with your wife or with your husband is the relationship based on an image, the image being the accumulation of many years of pleasure, sex, conflict, strife, boredom, repetition and domination; you have that image of her and she has a similar image of you and the contact between these two images is called relationship, and we have accepted that, whereas in point of fact it is not a relationship at all. So there is no *direct contact* between one human being and another; in the same way there is no direct contact with the actual, with what is.

Do please follow this a little! It may appear to be complex, but it isn't if you listen *quietly.* There is the observer and the thing observed, and there is a division between these two, and this division, this screen in between, is the word, the image, the memory, the space in which all conflict takes place, that

124

space being the ego, the 'me' which is the accumulation of words, of images, of memories from a thousand yesterdays, so consequently there is no direct contact with what is. You either condemn what is, rationalize it, accept it or justify it, and as this is all verbalization, there is no direct contact, therefore no understanding and consequently no resolution of what is.

Look, Sirs, there is envy, envy being measured comparison, and one is conditioned to accept it. Someone is bright, intelligent, successful and the other is not; ever since childhood one has been brought up to measure, to compare, so envy is born, but one observes that envy objectively as something outside of oneself, whereas the observer himself *is* that envy, there is no actual division between the observer and the observed. So the observer realises that he cannot possibly do anything about that envy; he sees very clearly that whatever he does with regard to envy is still envy, because he is the cause and the effect. Therefore, the *what is,* which is our daily life with all its problems of envy, jealousy, fear, loneliness and despair is not different from the observer who says 'I am those things'; the observer is envious, is jealous, is fearful, is lonely and full of despair, so the observer cannot do anything about what is, which does not mean he accepts it, lives with it or is content with it. This conflict comes about through the division between the observer and the observed, but when there is no longer any resistance to what is, then a complete transformation takes place, and that transformation is meditation. So finding out for yourself the whole structure and nature of the observer, which is yourself, and also of the observed which *is again yourself,* and realizing the totality, the unity of it *is* meditation, in which there is no conflict whatsoever, and therefore a complete dissolution and the going beyond of what is.

Then you will also ask yourself: what is love? We have dealt with fear, so together we are now going to consider this question of love. You know that word is loaded; it has been abused, distorted, trodden upon and spoilt by the priest, by the psychologist and by the politician, by every newspaper and magazine; they write and talk about it endlessly. So what is love? Not what should it be, not what is the ideal or the ultimate, but what is the love that we have, that we know? The thing that we call love contains jealousy and hate, and is beset with anguish; we are not being cynical, we are merely observing actually what is, what the thing that we call love is. And, is love jealousy, is love hate? Is love possessiveness, domination of the wife by the husband or of the husband by the wife? You say that you love your family, your children, but do you? If you really loved your children with all your heart — not with your shoddy little minds — do you think there would be a war tomorrow? If you really loved your children, would you educate them in the way you do, train them, force them to conform to the established order of a rotten society? If you really loved your children, would you allow them to be killed or horribly mutilated in a war, whether it be your war or somebody else's? If you observe all this, it indicates, does it not, that there is no love at all? So love is not sentiment or some emotional nonsense and, above all, love is not pleasure.

We must then understand pleasure. To most of us love, sex and pleasure are synonymous. When we talk about love, there is the love of God, whatever that may mean — and I don't think it has any meaning even to the clergy, because they too are in conflict with their ambitions, with their desires, with their authority and possessions, with their gods, beliefs and rituals — and there is also the so-called love that is implied in sexual pleasure. Also involved in love are anguish, pain and despair; so if love is not pleasure, then what is pleasure? Please bear in mind that we are not denying pleasure! It is a great pleasure to see those lovely mountains lit by the setting sun, to see those marvellous trees, that have withstood the forest fires and the dust of many months, sparkling and washed clean by the rain; it is a great pleasure to see the stars of an evening (if you ever look at the stars). But to us this is *not* pleasure, we are only concerned with the sensuous pleasures, with the intellectual and emotional pleasures. So we have to ask ourselves: what is pleasure? We are not condemning it, we are trying to understand it, trying to go behind the word.

Pleasure, like fear, is engendered by thought. Yesterday you stood in the silent valley looking up at the marvel of the distant hills and at that particular moment there was great delight. Now thought comes in and says how nice it would be to repeat that experience of yesterday, so thinking about that experience of yesterday, whether it was gazing at the lovely tree, the sky and the hills, or your sexual enjoyment, *is* pleasure. The image, living in thought with something which gave you enjoyment yesterday, thinking about it, is the beginning of pleasure; in the same way, thinking about what might happen tomorrow, the possibility that pleasure may be denied, that you may lose your job, be taken ill or have an accident, with all the worry and pain, is the beginning of fear. So thought creates both pleasure and fear, but to us love *is* thought.

Please, follow this very closely! Love is thought because to us love is pleasure, which is the outcome of thought, which is nourished by thought. The pleasure is not at the actual moment of seeing the sunset or the sexual act, but the pleasure is *the thinking about it.* So, love is engendered by thought and also love is nourished, sustained and prolonged as pleasure by thought, which if you look at it very closely, is an obvious fact.

Then one asks oneself: is love thought? We know that thought can cultivate pleasure, but it cannot under any circumstance cultivate love, any more than it can cultivate humility. So love is not pleasure, neither is it desire — however you cannot *deny* either pleasure or desire. When you look at the world, at the beauty of a tree or a lovely face, there is great delight, at that particular moment, then thought interferes and gives it time and space to flourish as pleasure.

When you understand the nature and structure of pleasure in relation to love and when you *realise it* — which is part of meditation — then you will find that love is something entirely different, then you will really love your children, then you will create a new world. When you come to that state, when you *know* love, then do what you will, there is no wrong; it is only when you are seeking pleasure — as you are now — that everything goes wrong.

• There is also the problem of death. We have considered what our actual everyday living is and we have I hope, taken a journey together deeply within ourselves to find out what love is, so now we are going to try and discover what death is. You will only understand this tremendous problem of death (not what lies beyond death) when you know how to die, and when you know how to die, what happens after death is completely irrelevant; so we are going to find out what it means to die.

Death is inevitable. The body, the organism, like any machine that is constantly in use, must eventually wear out, come to an end. Most of us unfortunately die through old age or disease without knowing what it is to die. There is the problem of old age and to us old age is a horror. I do not know if you have ever noticed how in the autumn a leaf falls from a tree, what a lovely colour it is, how full of beauty and gentleness, and yet it is so easily, so effortlessly destroyed. Whereas with us as we grow old — well, just look at us! The ugliness, the disfigurement, the pretensions! Observe it in yourselves! And because we have not lived rightly either in youth or middle life, old age becomes an enormous problem. The fact is we have never really lived at all, because we are frightened, frightened of living and frightened of dying and as we grow old, everything happens to us; so that is one of our major problems. We are, therefore, going to find out what it means to die, knowing full well that the organism must come to an end, and knowing also that the mind, in its despair at ending, will inevitably seek comfort and hope in some theory, some belief, which usually is resurrection or reincarnation.

You know, the whole of Asia is conditioned to accept the theory of reincarnation; they discuss it a great deal and write about it, and they have invested their entire lives in the hope and fulfilment of their *next* life, but they overlook one very important point. If you are going to be born again, surely it is very important to live rightly in this life, so it matters tremendously what you do *now,* what you think, how you behave, how you talk and how your thought functions because according to your actions in this life your next life will be determined; there may be retribution. However they seem to forget all this and instead talk endlessly about the beauty of reincarnation, the justice of it and all that trivial nonsense.

So we are not escaping from the fact through some theory, but facing it without fear. What does is mean to *die psychologically, inwardly?* In the death of the organism, there is no argument, you can't say, 'Please, wait a few more days until I become boss of the business!' or 'Can't you hold on a minute while they make me an archbishop?' You can't argue, it is final! So you have to find out how to die inwardly, psychologically. To die inwardly means that the past must completely come to an end — you must die to all your pleasures, to all the memories you have cherished, to all the things you hold dear, and *every day* you must die, not in theory but actually. To die to that pleasure you had yesterday means dying *instantly* to it without giving continuity to pleasure as thought. And to live this way, so that the mind is always young, fresh and innocent, always vulnerable, is meditation.

129

Once you have laid the foundation of virtue, which is order in relationship, then there comes into being this quality of love and of dying, which is all of life; then the mind becomes extraordinarily quiet, *naturally* silent, not made silent through suppression, discipline and control, and that silence is immensely rich.

Beyond that, no word, no description is of any avail. Then the mind does not enquire into the absolute because it has no need, for in that silence there is *that which is*. And the whole of this is the benediction of meditation.

17th November 1968

1

WE HAVE A great many problems, not only in this country but right throughout the world and they seem to be getting worse. One sees the necessity of change — economic, social, individual, communal and so on; also one sees that the more one changes the worse it seems to get. Obviously there must be a radical inward revolution, a total psychological mutation and we do not seem to be able to achieve this. There are all the specialists who say you must do this and you must do that, and the intellectuals who write innumerable articles, who, I suppose, are leaders. But I am afraid no one pays very much attention; we either accept or reject, we pick out the little bits that we like, hoping that somehow this wretched society will change.

First of all, I would like to say, if I may, that I am not a specialist of any kind, I do not represent India and its philosophy, its Gods, its meditations, its gurus and all that business. We are human beings, you and I, and we are trying to find out — not only what to do in the world, in the society in which we live — but also to find out for ourselves what it is all about, to find out for ourselves what meditation is and what is the way of emptying the mind so that it is vulnerable and innocent and fresh. Also, we are trying to find out whether it is at all possible to uncondition ourselves completely, so that we can look at life entirely differently, with a different feeling, a feeling in which all contradiction and all striving has come to an end. If we are alert to all these problems that confront us, then we want to know how to bring about the unity of man, so that there can be one government — not run by politicians, which, of course, can never be — where there can be a different way of acting and living, so that this division as the Hindu, the Muslim, the Christian, the Catholic, the Negro, the Chinese, disappears.

We have an immense and complex problem in front of us. It is not a problem outside of us; it is a problem that is part of us for it is we who are nationalistic, Catholic, Protestant — God knows what else! — communist, socialist and so on, all broken up into fragments, each accepting a fragment and living ideologically according to that fragment, in opposition to other fragments, to other ideas.

Being humans, living with a great deal of travail, we want to know what death is and if there is anything beyond the measure of the mind — not some mystical nonsense, not some invention of a shoddy little mind. We also want to find out for ourselves — if we are at all serious, purposeful — if there is a timeless state, if there is such a dimension within ourselves.

During these talks we are going to learn — not from me, the speaker has no value whatsoever — we are going to discover for ourselves the joy of coming upon our own intricasies; to discover does mean to learn and learning is a joy, not something painful; such joy releases energy; you must have that energy to go much further, much deeper.

If I may suggest, do not merely listen to a talk, to a lot of words and ideas; the description is never the described and unfortunately we generally get caught in the description and think we have found the whole thing. We must bear in mind that the word is not the thing, nor is the description the described. If that is somewhat clear then we can start to learn. Learning is one of the most difficult things. Book learning and the repetition of what you have learned from the book, in that there is no joy, no life; our education is based on that. The computer can do far better than the intellectually trained human being with his great deal of knowledge and ideas;

but we do not call that learning. Learning implies discovery, from moment to moment, so that each discovery about ourselves brings with it a certain enthusiasm, a certain joy, a certain quality of energy and the drive to find out more. All that involves the love of discovery and the joy of it.

So, we are not merely going to accept the description, but rather go beyond and deeper, seeing that what is important is the learning about ourselves, which is self-knowledge, the knowing of our ways of life, our motives, our demands, the attachments, the despairs, the agony and so on — to learn. In that way we are human beings that are discovering and not second-hand human beings, repeating what others have said, however cleverly, however logically or sanely. Such learning is not analysis; it is direct perception. You cannot possibly observe, have direct perception, if you have second-hand information about yourself. The second-hand information becomes 'the authority'.

We are not going to indulge in the analytical process — and this is going to be rather difficult. The analytical process involves time; I have to look at myself, analyse myself, find out the cause of my particular demands, neuroses, complexities and so on; through that analytical process I hope to find out the cause and thereby free the mind from both that cause and its effect. Is this somewhat clear? What we are going to go into demands serious attention, it is not a case of acceptance or denial, or a fanciful conclusion. We are examining and learning and learning is not an accumulative process. If one examines with the accumulation of what one has learnt, then the discovery of that which is fresh and new, is not possible because one is translating everything in the terms of that accumulation and one never looks anew and totally at this whole process of relationship and living.

One might ask: what is the difference between the analytical process, the professional analysis, and so on, taking months, years, and what you are talking about? The one involves a duration, time, the step by step examination of yourself by another, the analyst being also conditioned, like ourselves. We are not pursuing that particular method, or particular way, of understanding ourselves. I think there is a totally different approach to this whole problem of knowing oneself. Without knowing yourself you have no *raison d'être,* your relationship with another is merely the relationship between images.

To bring about a radical revolution in society — and there must be a total revolution, not economic or social, not according to the democrat or the republican, but a revolution that has a different structure and quality — there must be a deep and fundamental revolution in the mind itself.

The society which we have created is us; it is not a fantastic thing which has come into being through pressure and time; it is what we are, our greed, our envy, our despairs, our competitive aggressive spirit, our fears, our demands for security — all that has created this society. To bring about a change in that, *we* must change; merely lopping off a few branches of the tree which we call society — which is what is being done by the politician, by the economist and so on — will not change *us*. We are society; society is not different from us. *We* are the world which we have divided into — oh, so many fragments.

Life is for those who are earnest, serious, not for those who are flippant, not for those who are casually, occasionally serious, but who are consistently, purposively serious and earnest. If we are at all serious we see that there is no such thing as the community and the individual, there is only the human being who is conditioned by society, by the culture in which he lives; that culture and that society has been put together by man. So the question 'what is the good if I change, will it affect society?' has no value at all. What has value is to find a way (I do not like to use the words 'a way', it implies method, time, an end and all the rest of it,

135

but one will have to use these words, we will break them down afterwards) we must find a way of instantly changing so that our minds are innocent and fresh, so that tomorrow with all its agonies and fears has no meaning any more. So that is one of the fundamental questions: is it possible, living in this stupid, mad, insane world, not by going into some monastery, or retiring to some retreat of the Zen Buddhists and so on, but living in this world with all the turmoil, with its wars, with its chicanery, the politicians manoevring for their personal position and power, living here, is it possible to live a totally different kind of life, where there is love? Love is not pleasure, love is not desire; it comes into being only when we understand pleasure — and this is not the moment to go into that.

So, we are concerned with the human being, not with the individual. There is no such thing as 'the individual' — he may be the local entity with all his superstitions and conditioning, but that is part of the human being. We are concerned with freeing the human being from his conditioning, from the society in which he lives and which degrades him, a society that is perpetually at war, a society that breeds antagonism, hate, violence. So our question is: is it at all possible for us to change, not gradually, not eventually; when you use time there is only decay, there is only a withering away.

We are enquiring together, as to whether you and I, on the instant, can completely change and enter into a totally different dimension — and that involves meditation. Meditation is something that demands a great deal of intelligence, a sensitivity and the capacity of love and beauty — not just the following of a system invented by some guru. So all this is involved in an enquiry into life and death. You enquire when you have freedom, otherwise you cannot enquire — obviously. One cannot have prejudices, set conclusions, opinions, judgments and evaluations; if you want to discover there must be freedom to look. To look at things as they

136

actually are in ourselves — without finding any excuse, without justifying, lying to ourselves or pretending — is one of the most difficult things. Observation and the seeing of ourselves is one of the major problems — to see. I think we have to go into that question: what is it, to see?

When you look at a tree — I do not know if you ever do in New York — when you look at a tree, do you actually look at it, or do you have an image of the tree and the image is looking? It is not you, yourself, looking at the tree directly. You know, when you look at a cloud, at the stars of an evening or the lovely light of the setting sun, you have already judged it, you have said 'How beautiful it is' — the very statement 'How beautiful it is' prevents you from looking. You want to communicate it to another, but that very communication at the moment of looking prevents you from being actually in contact with the things at which you look. Is this somewhat clear? If you have an image about the speaker, an image put together by propaganda and so on, you look at him through the image which you have and therefore you are actually not looking or listening; you are looking and listening through a screen of words and images which prevent the actual perception of 'what is'. And that is one of the major issues in all our talks — how to observe. Is it possible to observe without the accumulated knowledge and experience: which is the past? Observation is always in the present; if you look at the present with the past memories — all memories are obviously the past, as knowledge is — then you are looking at the new thing with eyes that have been spotted with all the experience of the old and therefore with eyes that have become dull.

So that is the first thing, if I may suggest, that we have to learn: to be able to look at your wife, or husband, without the image that you have built through many years about her, or about him: and that is extraordinarily difficult. Our life is a series of experiences; we have had a thousand experiences

137

and all those experiences have become knowledge, they have left their mark on the mind, the very brain cells themselves are loaded with these memories and when we look at our wife, or at a friend or the clouds, or the light of the rising sun, we look with the memories of experiences, therefore the looking is of the past — with the eyes of the past we look and therefore there is no understanding of life as it is in the present.

To look demands a great deal of attention; I want to look at myself not according to any pattern, but I find I am conditioned heavily, I am a slave already to the specialist, my education has been directed, controlled by the specialist. If I want to learn about myself and to look at myself, to see myself as I am *actually,* I cannot do so without freedom, freedom from judgments, explanations, justifications. And this is not possible because my mind is heavily conditioned — by the analyst, by the society and the culture in which I live and so on. I look at myself with past knowledge and therefore I am not looking at myself at all. Now is it possible to put aside all that knowledge — technological knowledge, the practical knowledge, is necessary — is it possible to put aside the accumulation of experience, judgments and evaluations through which we look and for which reason there is never a change?

There is always a division between the observer and the observed. Relationship is direct contact, mentally, physically and so on; direct, not through a series of images or conclusions or ideologies. So is it possible to be completely free, free from your conditioning as Christian, Communist, Catholic, whatever it is? Otherwise you cannot possibly look, whatever you look at will be translated in terms of what you already know; change then becomes a struggle of conforming to the past conditioning. After all, conflict, inwardly and outwardly, is between two things, conceptual thinking and what actually is.

138

So, inwardly, the whole art of seeing and learning, and the joy and energy which are the outcome of that seeing, involves a tremendous challenge. That is, can the mind, so heavily conditioned by magazines, the radio, so many influences, can it break through? — not eventually but immediately. Now this involves attention; to give your mind and heart to understanding yourself, because that is of primary importance, that demands not concentration but attention.

When there is a radical change within yourself you are bound to bring about a radical change in the corrupt society in which we live. To understand oneself there must be freedom from the conditioning of yesterday and the projection of yesterday, which is tomorrow; today is only the passage between the two for most of us. Attention implies awareness, being aware sensitively. You cannot be sensitively aware if you have any conclusions, that this must be, this not be, according to an ideology. The people who have ideologies and principles and live according to them, are the most insensitive people because they are living in the future, trying to make the present conform to that. The ideology becomes the 'authority', whether it is the ideology of the Communist, Socialist or Capitalist and so on. So can the mind be free of ideals, of conclusions? — do please investigate, do find out for yourself why we have these ideals, this conceptual thinking, the Utopias and all the religious structures that have divided man throughout the world; they are all based on these conceptual ideologies and they are obviously idiotic, they have no meaning. And yet we indulge in them — I wonder why! Concepts — all thinking is conceptual, is it not? I think about something which has given me pleasure or pain and thinking about it, wishing it were or were not so, conforming to the pattern which I have set for myself, is conceptual thought. And one asks oneself: why do I live in the future, or in the past? Why do I look with all the accumulation of knowledge, which is me, which is words and

139

memory and nothing else? — why do I live according to that which is called tradition, culture and so on? — why? Most of us are totally unaware that we are conditioned. One is a Catholic, he is conditioned through propaganda of two thousand years — to me it is a most fantastic thing — another through 'words' as a Protestant, as a Hindu, as a Muslim and all the rest throughout the world. We grow up in it, we accept conditioning; but we do not live what it requires; we accept the verbal statement that we must love our neighbour, yet obviously we do not love our neighbour, we kick him, we destroy him in the office, on the battlefield and so on.

We are broken up as Christians, Muslims, Hindus, one system against another, yet knowing intellectually that these divisions have brought man such immense misery — the religious wars and so on — yet we go on. Why? Do please observe — why? What would happen if we had no ideologies at all? Would we be materialistic? — I am afraid we are materialistic, very, even though we have ideologies; ideologies are just playthings, they are of no importance in our life at all. What has importance is this constant battle of ambition, greed, envy and all the rest of it, that is what is real, not whether you believe in God, or this, or that.

Unless there is a fundamental change in what is actually in our daily life, we are not serious at all. And the situation demands serious minds, serious people, not lop-sided, fragmented human beings. So, are we aware of our conditioning? After all, our conditioning is the whole psyche, it is the background of the way we live, the thoughts, the activities, the feelings — from the psyche. (Love is not from our conditioning, but it becomes conditioned when we translate it in terms of pleasure — which we will go into, perhaps, another time.) So what am I to do? I know I am conditioned as a Hindu and so on; also I know that unconditioning myself is not a matter of time, not something I will achieve gradually. In the meantime, when I say 'gradually', I am sowing the seed of misery for others and for myself, for to have an ideology of non-violence and be violent all the time is obviously stupid. One may use the propaganda of non-violence as a political instrument but why does one have the ideal of non-violence? It is because of tradition, one has accepted it as part of one's life, as one accepts eating meat or going to war, saluting the flag; one accepts — and that acceptance has become habit. Can one be aware of that habit, aware, just to be aware that one is conditioned, that one has cultivated innumerable habits, just to look at them? Look at them freely, so that in that freedom the habits flower — see all the implications. If you condemn a habit you have choked it. If you say, 'I must not have that habit' you are caught in it, you have controlled it and it will not tell you a thing.

Can one be aware without time? Can I be aware of this conditioning, this habit, this accepted norm, the tradition, without saying to myself 'I'll get rid of it slowly, peel off layer after layer?' Is it possible to look so completely, without any fragmentation? To look so entirely, wholly, so that there is no division between the observer and the observed. Because in this division between the observer and the observed, in that space, in that interval, lies the whole problem.

Look Sirs, we live with resistance and conflict — that is all we know; and the resistance brings about a certain form of energy, as conflict does. Where there is conflict and resistance there is a mind that is broken, tortured, not clear, confused. Conflict — both inwardly and outwardly, in all relationships — is obviously detrimental, obviously destructive and yet as long as there is the division between the observer and the observed, the thinker and the thought, there must be conflict. When you say, I love somebody, is there not a division in that? for in that division there is jealousy, possessiveness, domination, aggressiveness — you know all the rest of it — which breed conflict. So, is it possible to look so that the division between these two, the observer and the ob-

141

served, comes to an end? — this is meditation. As to why this division exists at all demands a great deal of investigation, a great deal of enquiry into oneself. One of the reasons why it exists is because we are educated wrongly, because we have ideals, we conform to a pattern, respectability and all the rest. To find out for oneself why it exists — not occasionally, but all the time, in the bus, in the car, when you are talking to somebody — brings a tremendous joy. Then the observer is the observed — and he is more than that. And that does not mean that when you observe a tree, you become the tree — God forbid! it would be stupid to identify yourself with the tree. But when this division ceases you are in quite a different dimension — which is not a promise, which is not a hope. But to actually see this division disappear, for that there is neither the observer nor the observed, but only observation. For all this there must be peace and freedom — freedom from fear.

I think it is time we stopped. Are there any questions relevant to what we have talked about?

Questioner: How can we be free from fear?

KRISHNAMURTI: That would take a long time to answer. We will go into it next time we meet.

Questioner: (Inaudible on tape)

KRISHNAMURTI: I said, Sir, that observation demands looking — does it not? — to observe. There can only be looking when the mind is free to look and to learn about what it is looking at. Learning is a discovery and there is a tremendous joy in discovering; that joy gives you energy. You see, Sir, for example, the monk, throughout the world, has taken the vow of celibacy and poverty and obedience — God only knows why, but he has — and he thinks that by taking a vow of that kind he will have great energy to live the life of a

Christian or whatever it is. He does it, but he is sexual, he is ambitious, he is a monkey like the rest of us and he battles with himself inwardly. That battle within himself in a waste of energy; he is conforming to a pattern set by the church or by the tradition and so on and that conformity is a form of resistance; when you resist there must be a battle; and that does not give you energy. We are talking of something entirely different.

Most of us have very little energy because our lives are spent in struggle. In the office and at home we are driven by our ambitions, there is constant conflict, opinion against opinion and so on. And although that conflict gives a certain quality of energy, that energy is most destructive, as is seen in the world. In every office there is the competitive spirit, which, though it gives such energy, is creating a society where there are those who are on top and those who are below — so there is a battle. When one asks oneself: is life meant to be that way? — the battle between my wife and my neighbour, battle, battle, battle; is there not another form of energy which is not the outcome of pain, suffering, turmoil, anxiety, fear, guilt? There is, if one knows how to learn, how to look actually at 'what is'. One cannot look at 'what is' if there is no freedom — therefore one must be aware of one's conditioning. It is fairly simple to be aware, while you think this or that. If you can give time — time in the sense of chronological time — if you can give five minutes a day to look you will learn a great deal. You do not have to go to an analyst, unless of course you are terribly neurotic — then you are stuck. But most of us are somewhat balanced, perhaps not entirely, and to be aware of the imbalance — as you were aware of this hall when you came in, the proportions, the height, the light, the seats, aware of the people, the colour of their coats, jerseys, whatever they are wearing, the various colours and your reaction to those colours makes the mind highly sensitive. And you can look at yourself, all history is there and all knowledge, books then become quite irrelevant.

Questioner: My question is: a man spends eight hours a day cutting hair, or forty years of his life in an office — it becomes terribly boring; what is he to do?

KRISHNAMURTI: Think of a man spending forty years in an office — I don't know why he does it! *(laughter)* Young people are revolting against all this — to end up as an executive or as an office clerk — my God, they must be in revolt! Be aware of boredom, of why one is bored, go into it and one may find that one does not want to be a barber any more, or to struggle to get to the top of the heap — one may not want to do any of those things. One may want to be a real human being, not a machine; but find that out, do not allow oneself to be told in the papers and so on, find out the whole problem of boredom. Boredom invites entertainment, whether you go to the church to be entertained or go to the football — they are both the same. Find out what is implied in entertainment and in stopping it — go into it so vitally that you are cleansed of boredom.

Questioner: I have a concern I would like to share. All the awareness in the world cannot create a mutual relationship. I see that bishops always bless marriage and family life. Something in me, time and again, baulks at any approach which does not see something essential about mutual relationship. I find something essential about having mutual relationships.

KRISHNAMURTI: Agreed. If you have no relationship you cease to exist — right? Life is relationship. So we must find out what relationship is; I know we must have relationships; I know most of us are not related. We live in isolation; though one may be married with children, one lives in isolation in oneself, therefore one has no relationship with another. So, going further into it we find out what relationship is actually and what is merely called relationship. What is called relationship is the relation between two images, one which I have about her and another which she has about me, these images are the conclusions and the memories of the insults, the nagging, the domination, and all that. That is, then, what is called the relationship. Now, is it possible to have relationship without any of that? That is, to ask if love must always be a conflict? Is love an idea? — is it a form of pleasure which we have called love? To understand this problem — again we come back to the essential issue — I have to understand why I build images? My wife has insulted me, has nagged me; why do I have the memory of it? Why can I not die to it — die to it as she is inferring it, not afterwards? Is that possible? Never to have the gathering of all these insults, experiences, nagging — all that stored up. It means that one has to be extraordinarily aware at the moment she is being insulting, aware of the words, the implication of these words and go into it completely at that moment, not later — one has to be very sensitive, very alert.

1st October, 1968

145

2

WE CAN COMMUNICATE with each other fairly easily, accepting certain words with their dictionary meaning, listening to what is being said intellectually and agreeing or disagreeing. Verbal communication is necessary, otherwise we cannot understand each other. But further understanding depends on each other's intention to understand the word, for we may not want to understand each other in case we might have a great deal of trouble; or we might want to understand only partially, intellectually, without fully comprehending the problem — then we shall not act.

Communication becomes quite an interesting problem; the speaker may want to tell you something but you must be willing to listen, not only with the intellect but also with your heart, with your feeling — then there is a possibility of really, completely, understanding each other. But communion is quite a different matter. It is not something mysterious or mystical — as the churches throughout the world make out. Communion with each other is only possible when we have established between ourselves complete verbal understanding — knowing very well that the word is not the thing, the description is not the described — then the word 'communion' has a deep, full and wide meaning. When two people commune with each other, verbal expression may not be necessary at all, they understand each other immediately.

It seems to me, that in these talks, it is very important to establish this process: to communicate with each other as deeply and widely as possible and also to be in communion with each other. And that is only possible when you and the speaker are both intent, sane, with an intensity that is capable of meeting what is being said with all your mind and heart and in which there is no opinion, judgment, evaluation. After all, communion is only possible when there is some kind of affection. Have you not noticed — you must have — that when two people really love each other (which is quite a different problem and quite a difficult thing) there is established a communion; there is no need to say anything, there is instant comprehension and action. As we are going to discuss and talk over together many of the issues of life, we must naturally, if we want to understand each other, establish communion as well as communication. They must co-exist all the time so that one listens — not only with the critical capacity, with instant examination, seeing the truth or the falsehood of what is being said, neither accepting nor rejecting — but with the mind free to communicate and at the same time having this communion, so that you and I see the thing instantly and the perception is the instant action. That is what communion between two people means; there are no barriers, there is no sense of resistance or yielding, but of being subtly open to each other; then, I think, a different kind of action comes into being.

As we were saying the other day, our life is fragmented, broken up; you are an artist and you are nothing else; you are a specialist in a particular field and you know all about that and nothing else; you are a husband, with many problems in the office — as a lawyer, engineer, business man — you return home and you become the husband again, a relationship in which there is a cleavage, a broken state. Our cultures are different, our education is different; our temperaments, tendencies, our conditioning — though fundamentally the same — vary, as Catholic, Protestant, Communist, Capitalist, or as a business man or a scientist, a professor and so on. All our life is broken up and each field, as one observes, has its own activity, its own customs, its opposition to another field. If one could observe the facts in one's life one would see that one is brutal, violent, vicious and yet at home one may be kind and not want to hurt; one has a particular affection and at the same time one is afraid; one has ideals and concepts, which contradict one's daily life; one has innumerable beliefs and superstitions, which are at variance with daily existence. We can observe these obvious facts, we all live in fragments, in different fields of activity, all in contradiction with each other — perhaps occasionally touching each other.

When one observes the various activities of the different fields of one's life, one must inevitably ask if it is at all possible to bring them all together, to unify them, to bring about an integration so that whatever you do at home or at the office, *whatever you do,* is consistent, not contradictory and therefore not painful. That is: is there an action that is true and complete in all fields? I do not know if you have thought about this problem at all, as to whether it is at all possible to integrate, to bring together, to bring into harmony the contradictory actions, desires, purposes and drives of one's life. After all, one's life, as it is lived, is a series of contradictions and where there is contradiction there is pain, there is struggle, there is sorrow, misery.

❧ We are going to explore together — and that is as much your responsibility as the speaker's — to find out if there is an action which is always total, complete, covering all the fields. Any idea of bringing about an integration of two contradictory activities is obviously absurd; hate and love, those two you cannot integrate; you cannot possibly integrate, or bring into harmony, ambition and gentleness, quietness; you cannot possibly integrate violence and non-violence.

In putting aside the idea of integrating the various contradictions we see, nevertheless, that in it is involved the question of who is the integrator? Who is the integrator that is going to bring together, bring into harmony, the contradictory

148

drives, the contradictory demands, desires, the opposing elements? Who is it? For most of us, it is thought. Thought sees these contradictions and says, 'they must be brought together', 'I must somehow bring about harmony in all these fields' — and it seems that thought is our only instrument. Thought says to itself, 'seeing all these contradictions, seeing the struggles and pains', thought says 'perhaps I can bring out of this a great harmony, a great quietness'. *But surely thought has created these contradictions.* Thought, which is the response of memory, the response of accumulated knowledge, that very thought is a fragment. Thought is always a fragment because thought is the outcome of the past and the past is a fragment of the total time. Thought, thinking about tomorrow, makes the division between the past and the future. So thought, whatever it does, must be fragmentary, must always bring about division. And thought is obviously the 'observer' who says there are these various contradictory entities in me and I must act non-fragmentarily in order to live completely. Therefore the very 'observer' is the cause of fragmentation.

It is essential to understand these matters because for us thought is so tremendously important; and obviously, to think rationally, clearly, is necessary. But to wage war, to build an army, to divide the world into spheres of influence, into nationalities, into religious organized beliefs — all these divisions thought has produced. And yet thought says, 'unity is necessary', so it begins to organize various political groups, with their ideologies, or says there must be one world government. Thought, observing this fact of contradiction, within and without, proceeds to try to bring about an organized life in which it is intended that there be no contradiction; which implies conforming to a pattern of activity, to a principle, to an ideology — to follow, to obey, to imitate. Again, in that, there is a contradiction between 'what is' and 'what should be'. And that is the only action we know; an action that is

149

always produced by thought and that is always in contradiction.

Please do not merely — if I may suggest — listen verbally; but using the speaker as a mirror, actually observe this fact in your own life, the fact that we are slaves to thought; and the cleverer, more cunning it is, the greater value that slavery has — at least in the world. To go to the moon you must have organized thought; to kill another, thought must work at the highest speed. And thought has invented the innumerable ideologies and thereby brought about contradiction, division, separation; and that is the only action we know — the product of thought.

Now, the question is: is there another kind of action that has nothing whatsoever to do with thought? — an action which is logical, consistent, true, complete and has the quality of death and love — knowing that thought is always old, that thought cannot possibly produce an action which is completely new, for it is the response of the past, it can never be new, it can never be free. Is this clear? If it is clear that thought has brought about this division between man and man throughout the world and that however cleverly organized the world is by thought, it cannot possibly bring about the unity of man, then we have to find if there is an action which is not the product of thought. We must understand this, for when we talk over together the question of fear — which was suggested the other day — we must understand the whole process of thinking — completely.

Why are we slaves to thought? In certain fields of life one must think intensely, very clearly, rationally, logically, completely; otherwise all science would come to an end, all knowledge would cease. So we see that thought is necessary at certain levels and at other levels is detrimental. A mind that is conditioned by the culture of society, by education, by all the activities of daily life, is encouraged to think and to function in the field of thought. And we are asking a question which is quite contrary to our accustomed way of life. Now, how are we going to find out whether there is such action at all? — otherwise one must everlastingly live in this contradiction and misery. Because life is action, and although people may have made a division between activists and contemplatives and so on, yet the whole process of living is action — whether you go to the market, whether you read, whatever you do, it is action, and in that action there is contradiction. Is there an action that is always new and therefore always innocent, always fresh and young and alive, vital? If so, how are we going to find it? First of all, I am not telling you the way to do it — that would destroy your discovery; if I did and if you followed it, you would be just continuing thought, imitation, conformity and all the ugly business involved in it.

One must see very clearly how thought begins, what the origin of thinking is, what thought does in daily life, one must see how it separates every activity; one must be sensitive — please follow this — be sensitive to the activities of thought; that is, be aware — not resist thinking — but be aware of how thought is operating and thereby become sensitive to the whole structure and nature of thinking. Watch, be aware, be sensitive to thinking, to thought, without any condemnation or judgment — observe. And in that observation, in that awareness, form no conclusions, because the moment you have a conclusion you have ceased to be sensitive, you have already reached a point from which division takes place.

I do not know if you are following all this?

After all, Sirs, to be aware of the colour of the shirt of the person who is sitting next to you, you must be somewhat sensitive and open. Most of us are not keen observers, we do not even know how to look; we are insensitive because we are wrapped up in our own problems, in our own miseries, in our own anxiety and guilt, our demands, sex and a dozen things.

151

Where there is the continuity of a problem the mind must become dull. So one of the implications in this awareness is to end every problem, every psychological problem, instantly. Is that possible at all? A 'problem' implies something which you have not been able to solve, psychologically — we are not talking about the technological problems — the psychological problems which one has, which one carries from day to day, never examining, never questioning, over which we never become deeply concerned or involved. Is it possible to end these psychological problems the moment they arise? — otherwise the mind gets weighed down by one problem after another, it becomes very dull and insensitive and therefore watchfulness, alertness, this intent awareness without any choice, is not possible. Awareness means also, as we said, the highest form of sensitivity, which is intelligence. Intelligence has nothing whatsoever to do with knowledge; you may not read a single book yet be extraordinarily intelligent, because you are aware of what is going on in the world and you are highly sensitive to all the movements of your thoughts and feelings.

Where there is a sensitivity, which is the highest form of intelligence, when the mind has reached such a height of sensitivity, then what is action? — knowing that thought divides, limits. Then, that deep quality of the mind which has become highly sensitive, because it has observed the whole structure and nature of thought, is extraordinarily and extremely intelligent and this intelligence is complete action. Right? Has the speaker been able to convey this state? — not only verbally, but has he been able to communicate, commune over this fact, that thought is not intelligence? Thought, because it is always old, can never have this quality of intelligence which is always new, fresh; this intelligence which never divides so that there is an action which is never contradictory.

Questioner: Can you speak on fear?

KRISHNAMURTI: Unless we understand the nature and the structure of thought we shall not be able to end fear. Thought produces fear — as well as pleasure — right? When you see something that gives you pleasure — a woman's face, a sunset, a child's laughter — you think about it. The thinking about that fact — which for a few seconds has given you delight — is the development of pleasure.

I see a car, I see a woman, I see a lovely picture or tapestry; at the moment of seeing what takes place? Obviously — unless one is colourblind or whatever one lacks — one reacts. That reaction is either neurologically painful or pleasurable. Then thought — follow this step by step — then thought says; 'What a lovely thing that was', or, 'What a marvellous feeling I had'; thinking about it gives a continuity to that pleasure which you had for a few seconds; you think tomorrow about the pleasure that you had yesterday — look at the whole sexual act and image of it, the act, the pleasure and the thinking about it. So thought produces, nourishes, or gives continuity to a particular incident that has at the moment given you a delight — that is fairly obvious. And equally, thought produces or gives continuity to fear. I am afraid of what is going to happen tomorrow. Thought creates the image of what might happen tomorrow and is afraid of it. We will go into that a little more deeply, another day. What we are concerned with this afternoon is the understanding of this whole nature of thought. Until we are really familiar — not with other people's thought, not with the speaker's thought — with our own thinking, seeing how it comes into being, the nature of it, the subtlety of it, the structure, the design, the form, the content, we will not be able to deal with this question of fear. It is possible to end fear; it is possible, but only when you understand this extraordinary thing called thought — which we worship.

So, one must discover for oneself the origin of thought in oneself, the beginning of it (not a million years ago); as it begins, capture it and look, see where it has come into being. Then a deeper problem arises, as to whether the mind can ever be quiet, can ever be completely silent? — empty of all thought but extraordinarily alert. That is one of our major problems in life: seeing that thought has produced such havoc in the world, dividing the world into nationalities, into religions, into cultures, into all kinds of brutality, with all the saviours, churches, gods and the ideologies — all inventions of conceptual thought — can one break away from it? — for that is the only virtuous act, because in that there is complete freedom — (which freedom creates its own discipline). One has to go into oneself, exploring, being aware — not neurotically, not introspectively or analytically — observing the content of oneself as it flowers. I do not know if you have ever observed anger, at the moment it is taking place, giving it space so that it flowers, so as to learn all about it.

Questioner: May I infer from what you have said that there is something, some quality in man, that would be found immediately and rightly if the mind and its past did not get in the way?

KRISHNAMURTI: How would you answer that question? He asks: is there something beyond, in the human being, which comes into flower if thought subsides? How do you answer it? Please be careful. If you say 'yes', it may be your prejudice, it may be your hope; and your hope will then invent and that invention you will call intuition; and if you say 'there is no such thing', you are again in the same position. Both the positive assertion that there is, or that there is not, become unintelligent. All that one can do is to find out; to find out, to explore, to discover, not accepting any authority — there are too many authorities in the world all saying 'yes',

'yes', or 'no', 'no'. And the 'yes' people have led us up the garden path as well as the 'no' people. All that one can do is to find out; and when there is the understanding of oneself there comes into being the greatest form of meditation. Now is the understanding of oneself a slow process? — taking time, days, years; or do you understand yourself completely, on the instant? Do you see the problem? If you take time, gradually, step by step, learning about yourself, then see what that means? Every examination of yourself, each minute, must be complete, otherwise you carry it over and in that interval other problems arise. I do not know if you see all this? Either you learn, observe, know yourself through analysis (which is completely impossible because while you are analysing yourself there is an interval between the analyser and the analysed, the space in which there is contradiction, resistance and pain) or you see yourself completely, wholly, immediately. The latter is the only problem, the former is not a problem for the analytical process is no way.

Our question is: is it possible to see oneself completely, wholly, the whole thing, all the recesses, secret hiding places, completely? Is it possible to see the whole structure of the 'me', the 'self', the 'centre' — the centre that divides, that has so many tendencies, that has contradictory desires, purposes, anxieties, guilt, and fear — to see the whole thing instantly — for the very seeing of it instantly is the ending of it. To understand that, whether it is possible to see the whole structure of the 'me', the 'self', one must learn the art of seeing; just to be able to see, just to listen, without any agitation, without any conclusion, without any justification — just to listen. Have you ever listened in that way — to anybody? That means to listen with your heart, with your mind, with your nerves, with your whole being, not only now, but to every politician in the world, to your wife, to your children, listen to the wind among the trees — listen. In that listening there is great attention and in attention

155

Listen — as you try to judge + make conclusions.

there is no frontier. Then you do not have to take any drugs to expand your consciousness and play all those tricks upon yourself.

Questioner: Could you go into the implications of change?

KRISHNAMURTI: I must make it very brief. First of all, in this world, in the modern technological world, change is fantastic. So there it is, technological change. But there must be a total revolution psychologically and therefore socially. A man who has ten children, living in a slum, what chance has he to uncondition his mind and all the rest of it? None whatever! There must be a social change; but psychologically, inwardly, there arise two problems. Psychologically, there must be complete revolution, because as we are we are too greedy, envious, anxious, fearful, sorrow-laden — you know all that — psychologically we are that. That must change. There must be complete freedom from all that — complete freedom and therefore complete change in the structure of the very core of our being, our thinking and feeling. That is one problem. The other problem is whether there is change at all. Or is there an eternal mode, which is timeless, which we do not know, which we call change? I won't go into this for the moment, it is too complex.

Our major problem is: is it possible to bring about a change in one's life so that when one leaves this hall one is a new human being, innocent, fresh, clear, untouched by the contagion of time? — not as an idea, not as a hope, not as something ideological, but actually.

All this is implied in that word 'change', not merely an economic, social revolution, which does not lead anywhere ultimately — we have had Communist revolutions, other kinds of revolutions, they are coming back to the same old pattern. And one asks oneself whether change is dependent on circumstance, on the pressure of society, time and culture, or is there change without constraint and motive at all? That

156

is obviously the only change and it means that one has to go into the whole question of motives. To put it very simply: can one die to the past? Is the mind innocent and vulnerable enough? I do not know if you have ever tried to die to a particular pleasure, just to end it without argument, without fighting it, without resisting it, just to say 'it's over'. Have you ever tried? We want to die to a particular sorrow but never to a particular pleasure — but sorrow and pleasure go together.

3rd October, 1968

3

I AM AFRAID most of us are not very serious people; we are
inclined to allow others to think for us, to tell us what to do;
and that brings about a state of conformity, obedience and
acceptance. I think it would be a great mistake if we allowed
ourselves to agree or disagree with what is being said. We
are here to explore together, to investigate and to consider
together the many human problems that we have; just as the
other day when we went into the question of fear and
whether it is at all possible for human beings — who have
lived always with fear, with anxiety, with sorrow — to be
utterly free of it. But we have to consider fear from another
angle; also we are going to talk about time, love and death.
To understand what love or death is, we have to comprehend
— not intellectually, not verbally — the whole structure and
nature of time.

Most of us live in conflict; our daily life, as one observes,
is a battle-field, a constant struggle, a constant effort, a
constant expenditure of energy to overcome, to resist, or to
yield. In this there is the question of the opposites, resisting
or yielding; in both resisting and yielding there is conflict.
Our life is a series of conflicts and a mind that is in conflict,
in struggle, obviously is a tortured mind, a mind that cannot
possibly see very clearly, a mind that cannot possibly understand completely the whole problems of life and whether it
is at all possible to live in this world without any effort or
any conflict.

One sees that any form of struggle — in which is implied
violence — distorts the mind. One asks oneself if it is at all

Live w/ 'what is' and not 'what should be'

possible to live without effort and conflict, that is, to live completely and totally at peace, not only within but also without. To go into it, to talk over this question together, one has to consider the whole problem of duality, of the opposites, and whether there is any need for this duality, psychologically, at all. We live in a corridor of opposites, constantly being pulled in one direction or driven in the opposite direction, torn by different opposing desires, contradictions. Is it possible to live without the struggle of the opposites and, psychologically, is there an opposite at all? Or, is there only 'what is' and not 'what should be'? Is there only the active present and not the verbal or psychological future, which creates the opposite? If there are no opposites inwardly, psychologically, inside the skin as it were, then we eliminate conflict altogether, then there is only 'what is'.

Is it possible to see and live with 'what is' and not with the contradiction of 'what is', not with the opposite of 'what is' which brings about struggle, conflict, contradiction? Is this possible? It is really quite an interesting problem; we have to understand this question, because we have divided life into living and dying, hate and love, courage and fear, goodness as opposed to evil and so on — endless opposites.

The opposites breed time. There are obviously two kinds of time; chronological time and psychological time. There is psychological time, as not being or becoming — I *am* this, I *will be* that, I *am* violent and I *shall be* non-violent. The division between 'what is' and 'what should be' is the way of time. In that is involved becoming. I am violent and to become non-violent, to become peaceful, I must have time. The non-violence is the opposite of violence and this division breeds conflict, the conflict between myself as I *am* and as I *should be*. In that is involved the whole process of psychological time. And is there really psychological time at all? Obviously there is time by the watch, you have to have time to catch a bus, train and so on; but is there any other kind of

159

time at all? — for that time breeds fear. That is to say, I am vicious and hateful inwardly, I am psychologically ugly and thought projects the ideology of the non-violence that is to be attained, an ideology of perfection and so on. So thought involves time; and thought breeds fear. Thought breeds the fear of tomorrow — of what might happen; thought maintains the past as 'has been' and puts together the various possibilities of 'what will be'. Thought is afraid of the past as well as the future. Thought is time, and time, psychologically, is this division between 'what has been', 'what is' and 'what should be'.

We are dealing with the possibility of living so completely, so totally in the active present, that there is only the present and nothing else. And to find that, one must not only investigate the whole question of psychological time, but the way thought uses time as a means of achievement and how thereby it breeds fear.

We were asking: is there the opposite, the ideal? Or, is that merely a projection of thought, as a non-factual opposite of 'what is'; and does it not do this because it does not know how to deal with 'what is'? How does one unravel it and how does one understand the present?

Thought breeds the future as the ideal, and, as we said the other day, all ideals are idiotic, they have no meaning whatsoever, they have led man into all kinds of wars, inhumanities, division of people, hatred, various forms of suppression in the name of the State, or in the name of God and so on. Unfortunately, we have many ideals; they are the opposite of 'what is'. And because we do not know how to deal with and how to understand and go beyond 'what is', we resort to the escapes of 'what should be'.

Now, can we live with 'what is' and go beyond it, not inventing an opposite and thereby increasing the conflict, the misery, the struggle? One is violent, brutal, aggressive, ambitious, envious — that is the fact, that is 'what is', that

160

is the actuality — and all the opposites which man has invented have no reality whatsoever. Can the mind live with that — without the opposite — and understand 'what is' and go beyond it? Because to understand the question of love and death — which is one of the most essential problems of life — one must naturally live with 'what is' — actually. Can I look at myself, as I am, with my hates, anxieties, fears — all the innumerable tortures the human mind goes through — live with myself, understand myself and go beyond, without any effort? It is only possible when we eliminate altogether the opposites. Am I making myself clear?

Audience: Yes.

KRISHNAMURTI: Sirs, perhaps when you say 'yes' or 'we understand', you may mean verbally, intellectually we understand. Intellectual understanding is not understanding at all. It is like understanding a series of words because the speaker happens to speak English, therefore as you speak English also, you understand the words, verbally; but that is not understanding. Understanding implies — does it not? — the instant seeing as perception and action. It is as when you see a dangerous thing, you act instantly, there is no verbal intellectual argument. Here we have a very complex problem; all these problems are interrelated and complex, and they become much more complex when we deal with them intellectually, verbally. As we said, the word is not the thing, the description of the thing is not the thing described. What we have done is to describe and if we merely intellectually accept the description — the series of words which are merely conceptual — then there is no understanding and therefore no action. Action comes with understanding; they are simultaneous, instantaneous — you do not say, 'I understand' first, and then act. The very understanding is the doing. To understand is to live with 'what is'; which does not mean to be contented with 'what is', on the contrary. To understand is

161

to live completely with — let us take, for example — brutality or violence, which are spreading throughout the world.

Human beings are violent, in the family, in the office, everywhere in their actions they are violent, they are self-centred, egotistical. So there is violence; merely to indulge in an ideology of non-violence is obviously absurd and hypocritical.

Be aware that one is violent in different ways — sexually, in thought, in action; live with it, understand it completely. And you can understand it only when there is no escape from it through an ideology, through an opposite. If there is no opposite, how can you know that you are violent? Does not that question arise naturally in your mind? No? How do I know I am violent if I have not been conditioned to a concept of non-violence? Is violence conceptual or actual?

Is violence a word, a concept, or is it an actuality? When I am angry, the word 'anger' is not the feeling itself. Is the feeling itself conceptual, ideal? Certainly not, it is 'what is'. Can I, can the mind, look at that state of violence, not escaping from it to the opposite, can it live with it, understand it totally? That means that the 'observer' is not different from the thing observed, as is the thinker who says 'I am angry'. As long as there is this division between the thinker and that which is thought about, the experiencer and the experienced, the observer and the observed and so on, there must be duality. To eliminate conflict totally, altogether, means to live completely at peace within oneself, and therefore outwardly. That is only possible when there are no opposites, no comparisons, actively being aware of 'what is', the division between the observer and the observed eliminated.

If you are really concerned to eliminate war, anger, violence and hatred in the world — and every human being who is thoughtful, serious, must be concerned with this — if you are, how will you absolve yourself from this antagonism,

162

hatred, violence? It is a very serious problem and one has to apply oneself, work hard, to find out the truth of it. Psychologically, if there is tomorrow (and this is not a philosophical idea) if there is tomorrow, as psychological time, there must be fear and therefore violence. To be free of tomorrow is to live only in the active present; which means one must understand the whole machinery of thought, as the past and the future — thought which breeds fear, as it breeds pleasure. Unless you, as a human being, solve this problem you are inevitably contributing to hatred, to war, to violence.

I wonder what love is for most of us? Is love pleasure, desire, jealousy, self-concern? It is one of the most important problems of life and we must go into it rather deeply; we must enquire whether the human mind, including the heart and so on, can ever know what love is? Must it always live with hatred, jealousy, ambition, competition, and thereby eliminate altogether the thing called love? We asked: is love pleasure? Obviously in the western world pleasure plays an extraordinarily important part in life — not that it does not in the Orient also — but here it is so violently exaggerated and identified with sex. So when one asks this question: is love pleasure and therefore desire? We must also ask: what is pleasure, how does it come about? How does it happen that the mind is always seeking pleasure, like an animal, avoiding every form of danger, always seeking various forms of enjoyment, delight? That is not to say that we should not seek pleasure, that we should not enjoy looking at a sunset, the light on the water, a bird on the wing; the very look brings a delight if you are at all aware and sensitive — we cannot deny that. We are not saying that pleasure is something ugly, to be put aside. But we are enquiring into the nature of pleasure; because pleasure, for most of us, is identified with love, love of God, love of the country, love of your wife or husband, love of the family and so on.

What is pleasure? You see a sunset and it delights you;

163

the colour, the clarity, the beauty, the depth of light and the shadows in that sensory perception are instantaneous and in that there is great delight, great happiness; then, remembering other sunsets, other pleasures, thought thinks about the present sunset and gives continuity to that delight, which becomes the pleasure. Do please observe it, do not learn something as though in a class-room; watch this in yourself, in your daily life. You had an experience yesterday, it was painful or pleasurable; if it was painful you want to avoid it, put it aside; thought says, 'that is not pleasant, that is painful' and tries to avoid it; but if it was pleasurable, thought gives continuity to it by thinking about it. But thought, thinking about something dangerous, gives a continuity to fear. So thought breeds both pleasure and fear. This is clear enough.

Is thought love? Can you think about love? If you do, you think about it in terms of past pleasures, sexually or otherwise. So is love pleasure, bred by thought? If love is pleasure then thought is love — please follow this — thought, which is the response to the past, of memory, of knowledge, of experience, the past; thought is the response of the past and so love is then of the past. And that is all we know. When we talk of love, that is all we mean, a thing of the past, a thing that we have experienced as pleasure, sexually or otherwise. That is what we call love, in which there is pain, jealousy, possession, domination — all the conflict of relationship — and that is all we know. And when the so-called spiritual person talks about love, he talks about an ideology — love of God (I do not know what that means at all — do you?) — another invention, another worship of an ideology.

Is love or compassion a product of thought and therefore something that can be cultivated? Is it something that is rooted in the past and therefore never innocent, never vulnerable, fresh, young — something always held in the past?

164

When you say 'I love my wife' or 'my husband', 'my country', 'God' — whatever you love — when you say 'I love', you mean you love the image, the idea that you have built through time about another. Is that love? Or is love something entirely different, of a different dimension altogether? To find out something which is true you must deny that which is false, completely. In the denial, in the understanding of what is false, is the truth. Truth is not the opposite of the false; but it lies in completely understanding what is false, in putting it totally aside; in that is the truth. That is, to utterly abandon with your heart and mind, all jealousy, envy, brutality and the sense of domination and possession in which is what we call love — in denying all that, putting it completely aside, then the real thing is, you do not have to seek it, then it blossoms like a flower; without it, organize, legislate, do what you will, there will be no peace in the world.

To understand what death is one must know what living is. Is death the opposite of living? To us it is. Hence the battle, the struggle, the pain, the sorrow between living and dying. Perhaps, if we could understand what living is, then it may be that the very living is dying. We will go into that.

If you observe your daily life — and that of your friends and of your neighbours, of the world, of the human being — you see that what is called living is full of sorrow, full of struggle, frustration, anxiety — with occasional flashes of joy and an ecstasy that have nothing whatsoever to do with pleasure. Our life as it is, at home, in the office, everywhere, is a battlefield — we are not exaggerating, we are merely stating the fact as it is. When you look at your own life, the daily life that you lead, when you look at it objectively — not sentimentally, not emotionally — you actually see that it is hypocrisy, double-talk, pretension, struggle, endless sorrows and frustrations, loneliness, despair, brutality — you see that that is our life. And, of course, there is always God to escape to, organized belief which you call religion — which is not

165

religion at all but merely custom and habit and propaganda. So that is our life, that is what we call living. Then there is death, old age, disease, pain; that which we call death we want to put away, avoid and we cling to the things that we know, that we call life, everyday life. What we cling to is the sorrow, the anxiety, the pain, the misery, the confusion, the battle — but is that living? We have accepted it as part of our life as we accept so many things. We are more 'yes-sayers' than 'no-sayers'. We accept this living, this sorrow, with the occasional joy which soon becomes a memory and therefore again the repetitive continuing of that joy — which becomes another problem. So our life is a series of problems, frustrations, despair and hopes. And naturally we are afraid, naturally fear comes into being when we say all this must end. Being afraid, we invent theories such as that of re-incarnation. The whole of Asia believes in re-incarnation, to be born in a next life, to have a better chance, to be re-incarnated differently; if you believe in that, it means that you must live now righteously, it means that you must live this life so completely, so enthusiastically, so virtuously, so beautifully, that in the next life all that you have done now will bear fruit. But people who believe in re-incarnation do not do that. It is just a theory, a lovely concept, something that will give comfort to their petty little souls. And the Christian world has its own form of escape — the resurrection and all the rest of it — and if you do not believe in all that, you rationalize death.

So our question is: is there a way of living differently, not in this stupid corrupt way? Is there a way of living so that there is no sorrow at all — no loneliness, no frustration, no anxiety, despair — not as an idea, not as a concept, but actually to live in this world without comparison, without measure and therefore freely? Which means, really, one has to be so tremendously aware of one's own movement of thought, one's words and actions, that one's mind is never

166

captured by the opposite; therefore it is always living in the present; it means understanding the past, and the movement of the past through the present to the future. It means dying every day to everything that one has accumulated psychologically. Try sometime — do, if you will — to die to your particular pleasure instantly, completely, and see what happens. It is only in dying that something new can come into being. That which has continuity — however modified by time, by pressure — is that which has been; in that there is nothing new. It is only when there is an ending that there is a new energy, a bliss, an ecstasy which is not pleasure.

Questioner: I would say, if one has no pleasure, then one only has pain.

KRISHNAMURTI: If one has pain all the time, what is one to do? You mean physical pain?

Questioner: Well, I would say, psychosomatic pain.

KRISHNAMURTI: Psychosomatic pain — how does that pain come into being? What is the nature of pain? There is physical pain (toothache and acute disease) purely organic pain. Then there is the pain caused psychologically by various incidents: I am hurt, somebody has said brutal things, I feel lonely, I am lost, confused, there has been the death of the person whom I thought I loved, or my wife has run away, left me; all these contribute to pain, to sorrow, which affect the physical organism, as psychosomatic pain. And you say 'How am I, constantly being in psychosomatic pain, how am I to be free of it?' First of all, any person who gives advice of this sort to another is foolish. So we are not giving advice. We are exploring to find out why the psyche, the inward nature of man, why it should suffer. I recognize there is physical pain; either I put up with it or I try to do something about it. But why should there be psychological pain? My wife looks at another and I am jealous. Why am I jealous? Is it

167

because I suddenly find myself lonely, suddenly lose that which I have possessed, that which has given me pleasure, sexual or otherwise, comfort and so on? Also, it makes me face myself, see what I am, which I do not like to do; I see how petty, anxious and possessive I am. I do not like to observe what I am and therefore I get annoyed with the person who has caused this. Also it reveals to me how extraordinarily dependent I am. Seeing that, the actuality, not the image about myself, but the actual state of myself, is not a very pleasant thing. I will not accept 'what is' and I would like to go back to 'what was'. So I am jealous, angry, resentful and all the rest of it. So the family becomes an ugly thing.

The psychological pain comes only when I am unwilling to understand myself as I am, to face myself, to live with myself in my loneliness, not escape from it, to be completely lonely. And all my activity, my thought, breeds this loneliness because I am self-centred; I am thinking about myself all the time, my activity is isolating me in the name of the family, in the name of God, in the name of business and so on, psychologically my thinking is isolating. Loneliness is the result and to find out and to go beyond it I have to live with it, understand it, not say 'It is ugly, it is painful, it is this or that' — I have to live with it. I do not know if you have lived with anything so completely. If you have, then you will see that that which you so live with becomes extraordinarily beautiful.

You know, there is the question: what is beauty? I wonder why all the museums in the world are filled with people. Museums, music, paintings, books — why have they all become so extraordinarily important? Have you ever considered it? Somebody paints a picture and you say 'How beautiful it is'. If you have the money you buy it and hang it up in your house and you call that beauty. Probably you never look at a tree; or you go with an organized group to the woods to look at trees — you are told how to look at a tree! You go to college to become sensitive, to learn what it is to

168

be sensitive. How sad it all is, isn't it? All this means that one has completely lost touch with nature. It indicates that one has externalized everything. When there is great prosperity, without austerity, then there is the emptying of the inward state, therefore you have to go to museums, concerts, exhibitions — be entertained. And is all that beauty? Beauty goes with love and love comes into being only when there is dying. Love is something always new, innocent and fresh; it does not exist for a mind that is full of problems, intellectual concepts and struggles. Inwardly, one must live extraordinarily simply.

8th October, 1968

4

THE WORD 'PASSION' — the root of it — means sorrow. For most of us sorrow is something dreadful to be avoided, a thing that must be put away altogether or something to be resolved; not being able to resolve it, we either worship it, as the Christian world does, or, as it happens in Asia, give it some kind of explanation; they use the word 'karma', indicating that sorrow is the result of past action. But sorrow is something that is always with us, we may not acknowledge it, we may not be acquainted with it, familiar with it, but it is there. This sorrow may come about through frustration, through the sense of complete isolation, through the loss of someone whom you think you love, or it may be the sorrow of great fear unresolved. For most of us, sorrow does not bring about 'passion', it brings on old age, decay, a deep sense of utter despair, hopelessness. And one wonders — as you must have done, if you are at all serious about these matters — whether it is at all possible to end sorrow completely and come to that sense of deep abiding 'passion'. Sorrow does not bring 'passion'; sorrow, on the contrary, belittles the mind, clouds the clarity of perception; sorrow is like a darkening cloud in our life — this is an obvious fact and not a theoretical or psychological assumption.

One perceives the whole process of sorrow, how we human beings throughout the world have suffered, through wars, through uncertainties, through lack of relationship with another, through the lack of love; and when there is the lack of love then pleasure becomes all important. Not only is there this sorrow, but also — if you can observe it very closely —

there is the sorrow of ignorance. Ignorance exists even though one may have great knowledge, a good education, be sophisticated, have capacity in the exercise of which one achieves fame, notoriety, money. Ignorance is not dispelled by the accumulation of a great many facts and much information — the computer can do all that better than the human mind. *Ignorance is the utter lack of self-knowing.* Most of us are so superficial, shallow, have so much sorrow and ignorance as part of our lot. Again, this is not an exaggeration, not an assumption, but an actual fact of our daily existence. We are ignorant of ourselves and therein lies great sorrow. That ignorance breeds every form of superstition, it perpetuates fear, engenders hope and despair and all the inventions and theories of a clever mind. So ignorance not only breeds sorrow, but brings about great confusion in ourselves. Observing all this, one is conscious — if one is at all aware of the world and of oneself and of one's relationship to the world — one is conscious of this unending chain of sorrow; we are everlastingly trying to escape from it — we are born with sorrow and die with sorrow. We think that pleasure brings passion; it may bring sexual lust or passion; *but we are talking about a passion that is a flame that comes with self-knowing.* The ending of sorrow comes with self-knowledge; out of that self-knowledge there is passion.

One must have passion — but not identified with a particular concept, a particular formula for social revolution, or a theological concept of God, for passion based on concepts and formulas invented by a cunning, clever mind, soon fades away. Without passion, without that urgency and intensity, our lives remain rather shoddy, bourgeois, and meaningless. Our lives have no meaning as they are lived now — if you can observe yourself you will see there is no deep, abiding, rich meaning in the lives that we lead. We invent various forms of work, we invent purposes, ends, goals; if you are very intellectual you devise your own particular meaning within which to live; also if you are intellectual — seeing this whole activity of life, the struggle, the ugliness, the competition, the brutality, the endless torture — you will invent a formula and live according to that, at least you will try. In this there is no passion. Passion is not blind; on the contrary it comes only when there is the widening and deepening of the knowledge of oneself.

I hope you are not merely listening to a series of words; I hope you are actually looking, examining and exploring your own life, the life one has to lead — not someone else's life, someone else's concept of life, but the life we lead every day, with its boredom, routine, the endless struggles, the utter lack of love and kindliness, the life in which there is no compassion whatsoever. There is constant killing — not only the animal which we eat but also killing by word, by gesture, by thought. Out of all this there is more suffering — which again is not a supposition but actually 'what is'. We cannot escape from 'what is', we have to understand it, go into it, put our teeth into it, tear through it, and to do that we must have a great deal of energy. This energy is passion, and there is not that energy if we are in constant conflict. Our life is a dualistic business, a war between the opposites. And when there is violence, strife between the opposites — whether ideationally or actually — there is a waste of energy. You have energy — do you not? — when your whole mind is given to understanding; this energy is passion. It is only passion that can create or bring about a different society. We must have a different society, not this corrupt society.

Seeing all this, one wonders what will bring about a radical change in man. What will change you and me so fundamentally that we have a different mind, a different heart? This is not just words. If you begin to enquire into it very sharply, very clearly, you will inevitably ask these fundamental questons. Organizations, at a certain level, are absolutely necessary — the organization that delivers your milk, letters, the

172

government — however rotten it is. But organized thought is much more detrimental; inward existence that is organized by repetition, the following of a particular course of thought and action inwardly, becomes routine. The ending of organized thought does not mean disorder. On the contrary, if one begins to enquire, one will see that organized belief which is called religion, with its dogma, with its ritual, is not religion at all — is it? To go to church every Sunday morning, or whatever you do, and for the rest of the week destroy your neighbour, breed wars, divide man against man in the worship of hierarchy — all that is not religion, it is propaganda organized to make you think and act according to a certain pattern. All that is born out of fear; and how can there be a religious mind when there is fear?

I hope you are not merely listening to the speaker; that has no value at all because the speaker is not teaching you a thing, the speaker is not guiding you to think along a certain line, for that becomes merely propaganda and therefore a lie. But if you could use the speaker to observe yourself, then you will see that without having great energy and therefore great passion and intensity, life must inevitably be, as it is now, a thing of pleasure, entertainment and the accumulation of knowledge or things.

Organized inward movement, life organized by thought to live in constant repetition with an occasional break of the repetition, going to the office every day of your life — I do not know if you have observed — is ugly, sorrowful. And we educate the young to follow after us, to occupy these offices. And the organised morality — which is the respectability and the morality of acquisitiveness, of greed, competition, violence, brutality — we accept as moral. We may say it is very bad to be that way, but that is our life and that is our morality. Our minds, so organized, must inevitably be very shallow; however much you may accumulate knowledge the mind is still shallow, petty, concerned with itself, with its success, with the family, with its little activities — how can such a mind know either sorrow or passion? It is only in the understanding of sorrow that passion comes. So, seeing all this, not merely intellectually or verbally, seeing that this is the actual reality of one's life, what is one to do? What is your answer? This is your life, the ugliness, the growing old with all the ugliness of old age, the bitterness, the frustrations, the utter hopelessness of petty thought, the greed, the envy — you know, this whole thing in which we live — how do we get out of it? That is really the question; not whether you believe in God, or not.

Beauty comes with order, not when there is disorder in our lives. Beauty is not in the museum, in the painting, in statues, or listening to a concert; beauty is not in a poem or in the lovely sky of an evening, or in the light on the water, or in the face of a beautiful person, nor in the building. There is beauty only when the mind and the heart are completely in harmony; and that beauty cannot be gotten by a shallow mind that is caught in the disorder of this world.

When you are confronted with this enormous and very complex issue — what are you, as a human being, to do? When the house is actually burning you have no time to say, 'Well, let us think about it', 'Let us find out who set the house on fire, and with what, and whether he was black or white, or whatever it is' — when the house is burning you are concerned. So what are you going to do?

Change is obviously essential, not only outwardly in society, but also in ourselves. The change in society can only be brought about by change within — mere outward reformation, however revolutionary, is always overcome by the inward attitudes, thoughts and feelings; you have seen that in the Russian and other revolutions. So what is one to do? I wonder, when you are faced with this challenge, what your response as a human being is; is it to retire into some isolated monastery, there to meditate, learn a new technique, become a Zen Buddhist, or take vows of poverty, celibacy, chastity; or is it to join other groups of religious belief or sects, or play with psycho-analysis, or become a social reformer, mending the society which is breaking down? What will you do? Do, please, be terribly serious about it. If you cannot retire or escape — there is no way out that way, if there is no teacher, no guru who is going to help you, no organized religion, no God, for certainly God will not come to your aid, God is your invention — what will you do?

What does the mind do? What does one do when one is confused, as one is with this confusion brought about by so many specialists, by so much knowledge, with the confusion of one's own uncertainty and the seeking of certainty? What does one do when one does not trust anybody any more? — I hope you do not, — no analyst, no priest and all the rest of it. Inwardly, one has given faith to so many people — one's love, one's affection, one's adoration, one's trust — and they have all failed, and they must. So, when one is confronted with this immense problem and one has to solve it by oneself, without any help from outside, either one becomes bitter — which is the fruit of modern civilisation — or, what does one do? Are you all waiting for me to tell you? *(Laughter)* Do not, please, laugh it away. Are you waiting for the speaker to point out what to do? If you are waiting for the speaker to tell you, he becomes your authority, therefore you put your trust in the speaker, and if you put your trust in him then you will be substituting this particular authority for another authority and so you will be lost again; you will be destroying yourself.

So you can neither trust the speaker — please listen seriously — nor anyone else, any authority whatsoever; therein lies great beauty — not despair, not bitterness, not a sense of loneliness; you are faced with this problem and you have to solve it completely, yourself; in that there is great freedom and beauty. Then you are rid of authority, rid of the teacher, rid of the teaching, rid of following anybody, you are a human being free to look and to understand; in that there is great joy, there is beauty — you have thrown away all burdens.

The word 'responsibility' is an ugly word. We use that word only when there is no love; 'responsibility' is the word used by the clever politician, or by a dominating or asserting woman or man. But we are responsible — that is an actual fact — for everything that is happening in the world, the starvation in the East, the war — it is not an American war against the Vietnamese, it is the war for which each one of us, whether we live in the East or in the West, is responsible. I know you do not feel this. You may feel it for your son who is killed — and I hope he is not — then you feel sorrow-laden, somewhat responsible and carry on. It is when you love you feel responsible; not you love because you feel responsible. There is responsibility because you love; and free-dom implies responsibility, not responsibility for other people's actions — how can I be responsible for your action, for your thinking? — but responsibility for the action which comes with freedom. To be free without responsibility has no meaning.

You are confronted with this problem, and you are alone with it. Have you ever been alone? — alone in the woods, alone by yourself in your room — or are you always crowded by a horde of others, by your companions, wife or husband, by crowding thoughts, by professional problems? — all that indicates that you are never alone; and then when you are alone you are frightened. But now you are alone with this immense problem. There is nobody that is going to give you the answer. You are confronted with this immense problem, and therefore alone; out of this aloneness comes understand-ing and whatever you do will be right because that aloneness is love. That state of mind, that is confronting this immense problem without any escape, facing all the daily facts of life, the daily ugliness, the daily brutality, the daily words of

176

annoyance, of irritation, is alone; you begin to see the actual fact, to see actually 'what is'. Then, only, is it possible to go beyond it; then you are a light to yourself. That mind is the religious mind — not the mind that goes to church, believes in gods, that is superstitious, frightened; such a mind is not a religious mind. The religious mind is that state in which there is freedom and great abiding love. And then you can go beyond, then the mind can go to a different dimension and there is truth.

Can we ask the 'right' question? Most of us ask questions very easily. We must ask questions. To question indicates a doubting mind, a mind that is enquiring, a mind that is not accepting, a mind that is never saying 'yes', never obeying, but always seeking, learning. To ask the 'right' question is one of the most difficult things to do — which does not mean we are trying to prevent you from asking questions. But to ask the 'right' question implies a mind that is aware of the inter-locking problems of life and is *concerned* with the problems but not *committed* to the problems; it can ask because it has thought deeply, enquired widely; when it asks the 'right' question there is the 'right' answer, because in the very questioning is the answer.

Questioner: Do you believe in evolution? You have often said that understanding is immediate, the act of learning is on the moment; where does evolution play a part in this? Are you denying evolution?

KRISHNAMURTI: It would be foolish — would it not? — to deny evolution. There is the bullock cart and the jet plane, that is evolution. There is an evolution of the primate to the so-called man. There is evolution from not-knowing to knowing. Evolution implies time; but psychologically, inwardly, is there evolution? Are you following the question? Outwardly one can see how architecture has advanced from the primitive hut to the modern building, mechanics from the two-wheel cart to the motor, the jet plane, going to the moon, and all the rest of it — it is there, obviously there is no question whether these things have evolved or not. But is there evolution inwardly, at all? You believe so, you think so, do you? But is there? Do not say 'there is' or 'there is not'. Merely to assert is the most foolish thing, but to find out is the beginning of wisdom. Now, psychologically, is there evolution? That is, I say 'I shall become something', or 'I shall not be something'; the becoming or the not being, involves time — does it not? 'I shall be less angry the day after tomorrow', 'I shall be more kind and less aggressive, more helpful, not be so self-centred, selfish', all that implies time — 'I am this' and 'I shall be that'. I say I shall evolve psychologically — but is there such evolution? Shall I be different in a year's time? Being violent today, my whole nature is violent, my whole up-bringing, education, the social influences and the cultural pressures have bred in me violence; also I have inherited violence from the animal, the territorial rights and sexual rights and so on — will this violence evolve into non-violence? Will you please tell me? Can violence ever become non-violence? Can violence ever become love?

If we admit the possibility of psychological progress and evolution, then we must admit time. But time is the product of thought. When you say, 'Well, I am this today, a product of thought — but I will be something different next week', or at some future date, or tomorrow, that is a conception brought about by thought, obviously. And thought, as we have been saying, is always old. Thought can be changed, can be modified, can be added to, subtracted from, but it always remains thought; thought being the response of memory, which is of the past. And thought, the past, has generated psychological time. If there is no psychological time — and there is none — then you are dealing with 'what is', not with 'what should be', as thought. Again, 'what should be' is an invention, is an escape from the fact of 'what is'. Because we do not know how to come to grips with 'what is' we invent the future. If I knew what to do with my violence now, today, I should not think about the future. If I knew what it meant to die today completely, I should not be afraid of tomorrow, of death and old age, which are the products of thought, the conception of tomorrow. So, there is only one thing, *'what is';* can I understand that? — can the mind completely understand it and go beyond it? That means, not admitting time at all, because time is an invention of thought. So, to understand 'what is' I must give my whole mind and heart to it. I must understand violence; violence is not something separate from me, I am violence; violence is not over there and I am here; I am the very nature and structure of violence; that is to say, the 'observer' is the 'observed'. The 'observer' who says, 'I am violent', he has separated himself from violence; but if you observe very closely, the 'observer' is violence. When this is a fact, not an idea, then the dualism and division, between the 'observer' and the 'observed', comes to an end; then I am violence; everything that I do is born of this violence, therefore, effort comes to an end. When there is no division between the fact of violence and the 'observer' who thinks he is different, then you will see that the 'observer' is the 'observed', they are not separate states. And when it is seen that the 'observer' *is* the 'observed', as violence, then what is the mind to do? Any act on the part of the mind to do something about violence is still violence. *So, the mind realizing that whatever it thinks about violence is part of violence, its thinking comes to an end — and therefore violence ceases. The perception of that is immediate, not something to be cultivated through time, to be attained at some future date.* So there is, in that perception, the seeing of something immediately; in that there is no time or progress or evolution; it is an instantaneous perception and action. And surely love is like that, is it not? Love is not the product of thought; love, like humility, is not something to be cultivated. You cannot cultivate humility, it is only the vain man who cultivates humility; and when he is 'cultivating', that is, progressing towards humility, he is being vain — like a man who practises non-violence, in the meantime he is being violent.

So, surely love is that state of mind when time, when the 'observer' and the 'observed' are not. You know, when we say we love another — and I hope you do — then there is an intensity, a communication, a communion, at the same time, at the same level, and that communion, that state of love, is not the product of thought or of time.

Questioner: For most of us the 'what is' is an escape from a boring job, the society in which we live, from food reforming to clothing and so on.

KRISHNAMURTI: How do we transcend that? Is that it, Sir? How do we go beyond it? You have to earn a livelihood, haven't you? In the social structure, as it is, you have to go to the office or to the factory, either you conform to the pattern or you are free to conform or not. Sir, it is like this; war is the result of nationalism, the division of the superior and the inferior, war is the result of ideologies — obviously — and the economic ambitions of a nation and so on and so on — wars. Shall I, to prevent war, not buy a stamp, not travel on trains? Because everything I do helps towards war; the food I buy I pay tax on, also the clothes I buy, the books I read, everything leads ultimately, in the modern structure of the world, to some kind of violence. So what shall I do? — not pax tax? — become a pacifist? What shall I do? It would be foolish on my part not to buy a stamp, not to pay taxes and so on; but I can cry, shout, against nationalism, the flag, the divisions of people into religions, the Christian, the Hindu, the Muslim, the black against the white.

There is only one problem, politically, which is the unity of mankind. The unity of mankind is not brought about by politicians, they want to keep things as they are — separate — to achieve their own particular shoddy little ambitions. The unity of mankind will, probably, come about with a change of each human being's heart — the government of the world will then be conducted by the computers. Don't laugh, that is the only way out.

So, shall I not go to the office, not wear clothes and so on? So you see, Sirs, we want to reduce the immense problem by doing little things because we do not see the whole structure and nature of the problem.

Questioner: You say that if the observer is aware, that is the supreme . . . ?

KRISHNAMURTI: I did not say — please — that if the observer is aware, that that is the supreme; I did not say any of those things. If you are going to quote the speaker — and I hope you won't — you must quote him correctly. We use such a word as the 'supreme', the 'almighty', the 'immensity', the 'immeasurable', not knowing what it means. Do not use it. You can only use it with great seriousness and intention and beauty when you live rightly in this world, when you have laid the foundation of behaviour; then you will know what it means when you use that word 'the supreme'.

Questioner: What is one to do if one is incurably ill and suffers pain constantly?

KRISHNAMURTI: How am I to bear the pain, the fear of pain, the fear of death? If I have physical pain — great or little; when there is an awareness of that pain — please follow this; not the sublime something or other — just an awareness of that pain without choice, to be aware that I have a toothache, great pain, and not say 'I am suffering' and the rest of it, but being choicelessly aware of that fact, I will have pain, but I am dealing with that pain quite differently. There is not fear involved in it.

There is the fear of death from a disease which is incurable. Why am I afraid? Am I afraid of leaving my wife, my husband, my house, my memories, my character, my work and the books I want to read, the books I have written or am going to write — is that it? I am going to leave all that behind; and being frightened I create heaven, a hope — which again breeds further fear. So, can I be free of fear? I know I have to bear pain, a few drugs perhaps can help it, but there is the fear which is deep rooted, it is in the animal, it is in every human being, the fear of dying; and the fear of dying is the fear of living — isn't it? Fear of living: what is this life we lead with its ugliness, brutality? That is the only life we know and we are afraid even to lose that; we are afraid of the known and we are afraid of the unknown. We would rather cling to the known; and so we divide life into dying and living. We do not know how to live, we do not know how to die. When we know how to live, without conflict, with great beauty, with joy, and with clarity and passion — and that can only come about when you know how to die everyday to everything that you possess — then fear no longer is.

12th October, 1968